The Twentieth Century Atlas of Popular Astronomy Comprising in Twenty-two Plates a Complete Series of Illustrations of the Heavenly Bodies

THE TWENTIETH CENTURY

ATLAS

OF

POPULAR ASTRONOMY

*COMPRISING IN SIXTEEN PLATES
A SERIES OF ILLUSTRATIONS OF THE
HEAVENLY BODIES*

BY

THOMAS HEATH, B.A.

LATE FIRST ASSISTANT ASTRONOMER, ROYAL OBSERVATORY, EDINBURGH

THIRD EDITION

W. & A. K. JOHNSTON, LIMITED

EDINBURGH

GENERAL AGENTS: MACMILLAN & CO., LIMITED, LONDON

MCMXXII

112838

PREFACE.

THE progress of Astronomy during the nineteenth century has exhibited itself in two distinct forms, the march of scientific discovery and the increasing interest shown in the science by the general public. The discovery of the spectroscope and the application of photography to astronomical research have opened up new and intensely interesting branches of the science, while the older and more strictly mathematical department has been no less vigorously pushed forward. The second form of progress alluded to, for progress it must assuredly be admitted to be, would seem to depend for its existence on the first. The daily increasing interest in the study of Astronomy is doubtless due in a large measure to the rapid advances made in the science, and to the enlarged means of publishing, and above all to the improved methods of illustrating the accomplished facts as soon as they have reached the point at which they can be made interesting and intelligible to educated people who have not devoted special attention to astronomical study. That the general interest in astronomical study has enormously increased of late years is a matter which can hardly be called in question. If any proof of the fact were needed, it would be necessary only to call to mind the existence of flourishing societies, specially intended for the study of Astronomy by amateurs (amateurs in the best sense of the term), which have been founded, as well in Great Britain and the Colonies as on the Continent and in America. The hope of still further increasing the number of such amateurs is the prime object of the few pages which follow.

CONTENTS.

LIST OF PLATES.

CHAPTER I.

GENERAL APPEARANCE OF THE HEAVENS, AND FIRST RESULTS OF SIMPLE OBSERVATION.

To an observer viewing the heavens on a fine night, when the sky is clear of cloud, the celestial vault appears studded with stars of various degrees of lustre. If the moon be not present, the observer will also notice the Milky Way, stretching across the sky in cloudy patches composed of stars so small and so closely packed together as not to be separately distinguishable from one another. Astronomers have for ages recognised amongst the visible stars six classes or orders of brightness. A few of the very brightest are known as stars of the first magnitude; others, gradually decreasing in brightness, are said to be of the second magnitude, third magnitude, down to the sixth magnitude, the last comprehending a large number of the least bright stars visible to the naked eye.

A prolonged examination will further reveal the apparent revolution of the stellar hemisphere from east to west. The observer will soon notice that a large proportion of the stars rise from below the eastern horizon, cross the sky in curved lines, rising to their greatest elevation when they are due south, or on the meridian of the place of observation, and gradually descend till they are lost to view below the western horizon. He will see that the stars which rise on the exact eastern point of his horizon set on the exact western point, and that those stars which rise at points to the south of east set at corresponding points south of west. Again, stars rising north of east set at corresponding points north of west, and the farther north of east they rise the farther north of west do they set. Continuing the examination of the sky towards the north, it will be seen that the apparent paths of those stars which rise and set very close to the north point of the horizon are nearly complete circles, and a star may possibly be found which just touches the horizon at the north point, but which neither rises nor sets, and whose apparent path in the sky is a complete circle. If the centre of such a circular apparent path be looked for, it will be found situated close to a star of the second magnitude in the constellation Ursa Minor. This point is the north pole of the sky, and all stars situated within a distance of it equal to or less than its elevation above the north point of the horizon never set at our supposed place of observation, but describe circular apparent paths around it once in every twenty-four hours. These stars, which never set at a particular place of observation, are known as circumpolar stars. Hitherto the observer has been supposed to make his observations from a place in the northern hemisphere, but considerations corresponding to the above are of course true of the appearance of the sky as seen from a point in the southern hemisphere.

A

A simple method of showing the apparent motions of the stars in circles round the pole is to expose a sensitive plate in an ordinary camera pointed to the pole star on a fine night. The camera will be carried by the earth's rotation, and the images of the stars will fall successively on different parts of the plate, the result being that each bright star will produce a trail. Fig. 1 is reproduced from a photograph taken with an exposure of two and a half hours. The bright short trail near the centre is made by Polaris, and the position of the pole can easily be fixed. As the stars complete their diurnal circles in twenty-four hours, they will pass over 15° of these circles in one hour, or 37½° in the time of exposure of this photograph. This can easily be measured with a protractor. Fig. 2 shows the trails of stars near the zenith of Edinburgh, and is the result of half an hour's exposure. It will be noticed that the trails are still parts of circles, but evidently much farther from their centre, the pole, than those of fig. 1.

FIG. 1.

As we approach the equator the trails become more and more straight, and at the actual equator they are quite straight, as is shown by fig. 3, taken from a photograph exposed for twenty minutes on a point in the celestial equator.

Observations extending over a few nights will suffice to show the observer that the length of time during which a star remains above the horizon differs greatly for individual stars, and that this difference depends on the points of the horizon at which the star rises and sets. Thus he will find that stars which rise due east and set due west remain visible for half a day, whereas those that rise south of east, to an observer in the northern hemisphere will remain above the horizon less than half a day, and for a shorter time the nearer they rise to the south point of the horizon. Stars which rise north of east, on the other hand, remain longer than half a day above the horizon, and the nearer to the north point of the horizon they rise, the nearer their stay above the horizon will approach to a whole day. It will be found also that the circumpolar stars complete their apparent circular paths about the pole in a period a few minutes less than a day, as shown by an ordinary clock. This period, about four minutes less than a day,

Fig. 2.

is also the time in which every star completes its apparent revolution round the sky, above and below the horizon, and is known as a sidereal day. The difference between a sidereal day and the day of twenty-four hours, as shown by an ordinary

Fig. 3.

clock, will be explained more fully later on (*see* p. 10). Meanwhile it is sufficient to remark here that the interval which elapses between two successive risings of the same star, or two successive settings, is the same for every star, and is, in round numbers, four minutes less than twenty-four hours, as shown by a properly rated ordinary clock.

Another fact of great importance which will be noticed in a preliminary survey of the sky is, that though the stars at different times occupy different positions with respect to the horizon, they nevertheless always preserve the same relative positions with respect to one another. This will be at once seen on examination of any of the well-known constellation groups, such as Orion or Ursa Major. From the earliest historic times from which any authentic delineation of the constellations has been handed down to us, no noticeable difference of configuration is to be found amongst the constellations. For this reason the name of *Fixed Stars* has been adopted in contradistinction to the name *Planets* (from πλαναω, *I wander*), given to those bodies which change their apparent positions in the sky from day to day.

The Planets, like the fixed stars, vary in brightness. A few only—Venus, Mars, Jupiter, Saturn, and occasionally Mercury—are visible to the naked eye. Uranus and Neptune, as well as all the minor planets, can be seen only with telescopic assistance. If the planets are observed from night to night it will be found that they have, in common with the fixed stars, an apparent diurnal motion, by virtue of which they rise in the east, attain their highest point above the horizon when due south, and set in the west. They have also, however, in addition, an apparent motion amongst the fixed stars, which cannot long escape the eye of the careful observer. It will readily be seen that the general direction of their paths amongst the stars is towards the east, but that this easterly course occasionally gives place to a movement in the opposite direction, lasting for a comparatively short period. On the whole their movement is towards the east, and in this direction they pass from constellation to constellation, making a complete tour of the heavens in a period which differs largely for each planet. When easterly, the movement of the planets amongst the stars is said to be *direct;* when westerly, it is called *retrograde.*

CHAPTER II.

THAT the figure of the earth approaches very closely that of a sphere or globe is so obvious from many considerations that it has been known from a very early period in the history of astronomy. The well-known fact of the gradual disappearance of the hull of a ship when sailing out to sea, before the rigging and masts, can only be explained on the supposition that the earth is round. The outline of the earth's shadow, caused by the interception of the sun's light by the opaque body of the earth, as seen in lunar eclipses, is always found to be circular—a circumstance which could happen only if the shadow were formed by a globular body. Since, however, the circumnavigation of the earth has become an accomplished fact, further proof of its rotundity is scarcely needed, except as a matter of interest to the student.

It would be foreign to the purpose of these pages to enter into an account of the astronomical systems and theories accepted by the ancients. The Ptolemaic system, which supposed that the earth was the centre round which all the heavenly bodies revolved, was only removed from scientific belief when the simpler and more natural ideas of Copernicus were introduced. This astronomer, who lived 1473-1543, was led to doubt the truth of the Ptolemaic system when he noticed that the planet Mars differed very much in brilliance under different circumstances, being sometimes the brightest star in the heavens, sometimes less bright than a fourth magnitude star. He argued that this could not be the case if Mars revolved in a circle about the earth as centre. He was thus led to consider the case of the other planets, and finally came to the conclusion that the earth was itself a planet, and that it as well as the others, revolved in orbits of greater or less extent around the sun. He was further forced to the conclusion that the apparent daily movement of the stars and planets from east to west was only to be explained by the rotation of the earth on an axis in the contrary direction, or from west to east.

It is important that the student of astronomy should have a distinct understanding of the method by which astronomers habitually fix the position of the heavenly bodies in the celestial sphere. On the earth's surface positions of places are fixed by the adoption of circles of latitude and longitude. That circle on the terrestrial globe, the plane of which passes through the centre of the earth, and is at right angles to the axis of rotation, is called the *Equator*. All points on this circle are equidistant from the extremities of the axis of rotation, the north and south poles. Each of these poles is thus distant 90° from all points of the equator. Circles parallel to the equator are called circles of latitude, and circles drawn through the poles and perpendicular to the equator are called meridians.

Latitude of any point on a terrestrial globe is thus its angular distance from the equator, measured by the arc of the meridian intercepted between the point and the equator, or by the angle subtended by this arc at the centre of the earth. Longitude is the angular distance, measured along the equator, between the points where the meridians, passing through the place and through the zero of longitude cut the equator. In the British Empire the meridian of Greenwich has been adopted as the zero, or starting meridian for longitudes, and these are measured east and west from 0° to 180°, or half way round the globe in each direction. In France the meridian of Paris is used for this purpose. As the earth rotates on its axis in 24 hours, or through an angle of 15° in 1 hour, longitudes may be measured from 0 to 12 hours east or west.

To determine, with a considerable degree of accuracy, the direction of the north and south points of the horizon at any place, or the points where the meridian of the place cuts the horizon on the north and south, the following method may be adopted. Set up a straight stick of any convenient length in a vertical position on a horizontal surface. Draw a circle of suitable radius having its centre at the foot of the stick. Mark the exact spot where the shadow caused by the interception of the sun's light by the top of the stick cuts the circle in the forenoon, and again in the afternoon ; bisect the part of the circle between these two points and you have the north point on the circle. The opposite point of the circle is the south. In practice, two or three concentric circles should be drawn, and each of them marked in the forenoon and afternoon. We have thus several determinations of the north and south points, from which a more accurate result can be obtained than from a single observation.

The direction of the north and south points can also be found by means of the magnetic compass needle, but this method requires a knowledge of the exact amount of what is called variation of the compass at the place ; the result is also liable to error from the presence of iron in quantity in the vicinity. The magnetic needle does not generally point to the true or geographical north, but to a point which, for the British Isles, is considerably to the west of north, the variation differing greatly with locality. This arises from the fact that the earth is itself a magnet. If the poles of the terrestrial magnet were situated at the north and south poles of the earth, the needle would be attracted towards them, and would invariably point north or south. This, however, is not the case, the needle being attracted to two points in the northern hemisphere, situated in the north of the American continent and in Northern Siberia respectively, and to two corresponding points in the southern hemisphere. The direction of the needle in the northern hemisphere, therefore, depends on the situation of the place of observation with respect to the American and Siberian foci of attraction. A freely suspended magnetic needle will take up its position of rest more or less in the direction of one or other of these foci, according as it is more or less strongly attracted by one or by the other. The variation of the needle from the direction of the true or geographical north, or the declination, as it is often called, is there- fore a matter for actual observation. Magnetic surveys of many portions of the globe have been made, and maps have been constructed showing lines of equal variation or declination. Fig. 4 shows approximately the amount of variation of the magnetic needle for all places in the British Isles for the year 1910, and has been prepared partly from the " Magnetic Survey " of Professor Rücker and Dr Thorpe, published in the *Philosophical Transactions* for 1896, and partly from more recent observations. The curved lines show the mean variation or declination, but considerable local deviations exist, and should be taken into

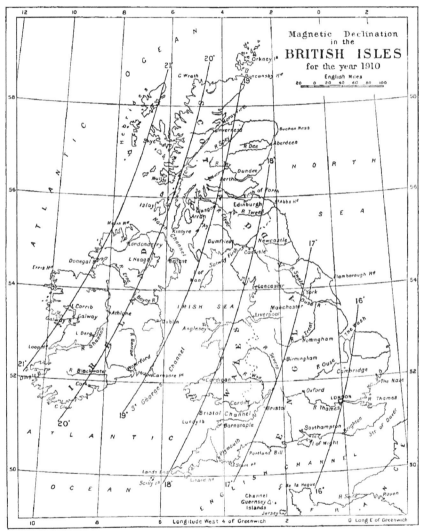

FIG. 4

account when extreme accuracy is desired. The amount of these deviations will be found in the *Philosophical Transactions* for 1896, on map No. 9, for a large number of stations throughout the British Isles. They are largest in the islands off the west coast of Scotland, and in the districts round Malvern, Birmingham, and Derby. In Ireland the deviations are small, except in the extreme west and in the north-east. The variation is in a state of slow but constant change, gradually lessening in the British Isles by an amount which varies somewhat in different parts of the country. The curved lines in the figure show where the declination is the same, and its approximate value in 1910 is given in degrees. Knowing the variation, we must lay down the direction taken by the needle at rest. This for Great Britain will be west of north. Hence we have only to draw a line making with the direction of the needle an angle equal to the variation at the place; this latter will point to the true or geographical north.

Plate I., fig. 1., should be studied carefully with reference to the following considerations. As the apparent diurnal motion of the stars across the sky from east to west is caused by the real rotation of the earth on its axis from west to east, we can fix the positions of the stars on the celestial sphere in a manner precisely analagous to that by which positions of points on the earth's surface are denoted. An imaginary counterpart of each one of the circles of the terrestrial sphere, to which allusion has just been made, can be produced on the face of the sky. Thus, the plane of the terrestrial equator produced in every direction intersects the sky in the celestial equator or equinoctial circle. The earth's axis of rotation produced intersects the sky in two points, the north and south poles of the heavens, the points about which the stars appear to revolve in their diurnal paths. The planes of the terrestrial meridians produced cut the sky in great circles, which pass through the north and south poles of the heavens, and are at right angles to the celestial equator. The declination of a heavenly body is its angular distance from the equator measured along such a meridian; while its right ascension is the angle between two meridians, one passing through the heavenly body and the other through the zero, or starting-point of right ascensions, which is the intersection of the ecliptic with the equinoctial, known as the "first point of Aries." The ecliptic may be defined as the plane of the earth's orbit round the sun produced in all directions, or as the great circle in the heavens which the sun appears to traverse in its annual course amongst the fixed stars. The plane of this great circle passes through the earth's centre, and is inclined at an angle of about $23\frac{1}{2}°$ to the plane of the equator. This angle is known as the "obliquity of the ecliptic," and is subject to a very small and slow decrease in its amount. Its value at the beginning of the nineteenth century was $23° 27' 55''$; it is now (1922) $23° 26' 58''$.

The place of a star can also be fixed by its latitude and longitude, referred to the ecliptic. Its latitude is its angular distance from the ecliptic measured on a great circle perpendicular to the ecliptic; while its longitude is reckoned along the ecliptic from the first point of Aries. The latitude and longitude of a celestial object must not be confounded with the same terms applied to a place on the earth's surface. Terrestrial latitude and longitude are more nearly analogous to the declination and right ascension of a celestial object, all these being referred to the equinoctial.

The two great planes of the equator and the ecliptic intersect one another along a straight line passing through the earth's centre. The two opposite points where this line cuts the sky are known as the "first point of Aries" and the "first point of Libra." The sun in its annual course round the ecliptic arrives at the former of these points on the 21st of March of each year, at the Spring or Vernal Equinox, and at the latter point on the 23rd of September, the Autumnal Equinox. The equinoxes are so called because the sun being also then momentarily in the equator, day and night are equal all over the world. At the vernal equinox the sun crosses the equator from south to north. The point on the celestial concave at which the sun then is has been adopted universally as the starting-point for measuring the right ascensions of the heavenly bodies. The whole circle of the ecliptic has been divided into twelve equal parts or signs, each of 30°, called after the constellations situated nearest to them at the time when the names were affixed to them. Owing to the phenomenon known as the precession of the equinoxes, referred to later at p. 22, the signs are not now coincident with the constellations whose names they still bear. The first point of Aries has shifted back into the constellation Pisces, and the first point of Libra into the constellation Virgo. The names of the signs in their order, and the approximate dates at which the sun enters them, are as follows :—

♈	ARIES, the Ram	. .	March	21	Spring Equinox.
♉	TAURUS, the Bull	. .	April	20	
♊	GEMINI, the Twins	. .	May	21	
♋	CANCER, the Crab	. .	June	22	Summer Solstice.
♌	LEO, the Lion	. . .	July	23	
♍	VIRGO, the Virgin	. .	Aug.	23	
♎	LIBRA, the Balance	. .	Sept.	23	Autumnal Equinox.
♏	SCORPIO, the Scorpion	.	Oct.	24	
♐	SAGITTARIUS, the Archer	.	Nov.	22	
♑	CAPRICORNUS, the Goat	.	Dec.	22	Winter Solstice.
♒	AQUARIUS, the Water Carrier		Jan.	20	
♓	PISCES, the Fishes	. .	Feb.	19	

The name Zodiac was given to the belt of the sky 8° or 9° on each side of the ecliptic, because the majority of the figures of the constellations in it are animals, real or mythical. It is in this region of the sky that the movements of the sun, moon, and the greater planets appear to take place. Hence the importance attached to it in old systems of astronomy. Of the planets, the more conspicuous ones only were known to the ancients. Many of the minor planets discovered in modern times do not confine their movements to the constellations of the Zodiac. Indeed, the use of the signs as a division of the Zodiac for indicating the positions of the sun, moon, or planets has now become obsolete, the name "first point of Aries" being the sole remnant of the method now retained for the purposes of practical astronomy. In consequence of the retrograde movement of the first point of Aries along the ecliptic, the constellations of the Zodiac should be distinguished from the signs of the Zodiac bearing the same names.

CHAPTER III.

TIME.

THE determination of true time is one of the most obvious practical applications of the study of astronomy. Those natural phenomena which are most intimately associated with human life, and which are regularly periodical in their recurrence, must necessarily be adopted as the units by which time is measured. The consecutive alternations of light and darkness, depending on the rotation of the earth on its axis, and the vicissitudes of the seasons, resulting from the revolution of the earth in its orbit around the sun, are the phenomena which stand out most conspicuously in regulating the affiairs of mankind. Hence amongst all nations the day and the year have been universally adopted as the units of time. A unit of measurement to be serviceable must be invariable. If we define the day as the interval which elapses between two consecutive returns of the sun to the meridian of the same place, we are at once confronted with the difficulty arising from the fact that this interval is not always the same, but is subject to gradual fluctuations throughout the course of the year. Thus this interval, at its maximum near the end of December, gradually decreases day by day till the end of March, after which it increases again to the middle of June. From this point to the middle of September it decreases, and again increases till it attains its maximum before the end of December. It is impossible therefore to make use of the apparent solar day—that is, the interval between two consecutive appearances of the sun on the meridian—as a measure of time. But the difficulty has been surmounted by the adoption of a *mean* solar day, whose length is equal to the average of the lengths of all the *apparent* solar days in the year. The mean solar day is divided into twenty-four hours of mean time, shown for practical purposes on the ordinary clocks in use amongst all civilised nations.

The mean solar day, though depending on the rotation of the earth on its axis, is not a measure of the duration of this rotation. The time which elapses between two consecutive appearances of the same point of the celestial concave, such as the position of a fixed star, on the meridian of any place, is an exact equivalent of this rotation, and is known as a sidereal day. The sidereal day is more accurately defined as the interval between two successive passages of the first point of Aries across the meridian of any place on the earth's surface. The difference between the two definitions arises from the very small daily effect of precession, an affect so small that it may be neglected here. This day is also divided into twenty-four hours, and the sidereal time thus defined is shown on clocks in constant use among astronomers for the purposes of practical astronomy. These clocks are made to show o hours o minutes o seconds at the moment when the first point of Aries is on the meridian of the observatory.

The inequalities in the length of the apparent solar day arise from two causes: (1) the variable motion of the sun in the ecliptic or of the earth in its orbit ; (2) from the fact that the earth's access of rotation is not at right angles to the plane of the ecliptic. The earth revolves about the sun in an elliptic orbit, having the sun in one of the foci, and in accordance with the dynamical laws of such motion the imaginary line joining the earth and sun sweeps over equal areas in equal times. But the earth being farther from the sun in summer than in winter, the areas can be equal only if the angles swept over are less, when the distance is greater. Suppose A B, fig. 5, to represent the earth's motion in its orbit during, say, ten days in July, and C D during ten days in January, the distances A S and B S are greater than C S and D S, hence the areas B S A and D S C can only be equal if the angle B S A is less than the angle D S C. The motion of the earth in its orbit is thus less rapid at B A than at C D, and the motion of the sun as seen from these positions, projected on the celestial conclave, must vary similarly. If the sun's motion were equable there would still be an inequality in the length of the apparent solar day, due to the second cause referred to—the inclination of the equator to the ecliptic. From this inclination it follows that equal arcs on the ecliptic do not measure equal arcs on the equator, and it is by these latter arcs, or

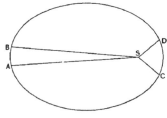

FIG. 5.

the angles they subtend at the pole, that time is measured. The difference between the apparent solar day and the mean solar day, resulting from these two causes, is known as the equation of time.

This quantity varies considerably in the course of the year, each of its components changing its value independently. It will help somewhat to understand this matter if we suppose a sun moving, not with varying motion in the ecliptic as the real sun does, but uniformly in the equator. Such an imaginary sun would cross the meridian of any place at intervals of twenty-four hours of mean solar time, and its meridian passage would take place at noon of the local mean time of that place. An ordinary clock would follow its movements from day to day throughout the year, and there would be no equation of time required. Now, let us compare the movements of this fictitious sun with those of the real sun, and let us consider first that portion of the equation of time which results from the obliquity of the ecliptic. If we could start the two suns together from the first point of Aries, the vernal equinox, the fictitious sun would move towards the east along the equator, increasing its right ascension daily by an average amount of 59' 8" of arc, or 3 minutes 56 seconds of time—these numbers being found by dividing 360°, or 24 hours, by the number of days in a year. The real sun, which, as we are at present considering only the obliquity, we may suppose for the moment to move uniformly in the ecliptic with an average daily motion of 59′ 8″, is now moving obliquely to the equator. Its average daily motion would therefore carry it to a point in the ecliptic through which, if we draw a meridian from the pole to the equator, it would meet the latter circle at a point short of the position our fictitious sun has reached by its average daily motion, or the fictitious sun would be east of the real sun. But the meridian of a place is carried by the earth's rotation from west to east across the sky, and would thus reach the westerly object, the real sun, before it reached the fictitious sun, or apparent noon would take place before mean noon. There would thus be, from the vernal equinox, an equation, due to the obliquity of the ecliptic, to be subtracted from apparent time. This equation with the minus sign increases up to the end of April, and then falls off to nothing at the summer solstice. At this point the fictitious sun, moving uniformly in the equator, and the real sun, which we still suppose to move uniformly in the ecliptic, are again together on the meridian, each having moved over 90° of their annual paths. From the summer solstice to the autumnal equinox there is a similar equation to be added to apparent time. From thence to the winter solstice it is again to be subtracted, and from this point to the vernal equinox it is to be added. There are thus four dates in the course of the year when this part of the equation of time is zero, and at which it alters from additive to subtractive, or *vice versa*—the two equinoxes and the two solstices.

To explain the other component of the equation of time—that which arises from the varying motion of the sun in the ecliptic—we can compare the motion of the real sun with that of a fictitious sun moving uniformly in the ecliptic with the average daily motion of the real sun. At the time of perihelion, in the beginning of January, the earth is moving rapidly in its orbit, and the sun appears to move rapidly in the ecliptic, the daily rate of motion at this time of the year being about 1° 1′ 9″, whereas at aphelion it is only 57′ 11″. Hence if the two suns were to start together at perihelion, after a day the real sun would be to the east of the fictitious, and therefore the latter would pass the meridian before the former, or mean noon would occur before apparent noon. The equation due to this cause is to be added to apparent time. It increases to a maximum about the 1st April, and gradually decreases to nothing at the time of aphelion, about the 1st July, when the real and fictitious suns would be together again, each of them having passed over 180° of its annual path. From aphelion to perihelion the equation would be subtracted from apparent time, and it would increase up to 1st October, and afterwards decrease to nothing at perihelion. For this part of the equation there are only two dates at which it is zero—the days of perihelion and aphelion. The equation of time as given in the almanacs is a combination of these two components for each day, with their proper signs, and it will be found that there are four days in the year—16th April, 15th June, 1st September, and 25th December—when it is zero. Apparent time, as shown by a sun-dial, is, on these days, the same as the time shown by a clock set to *local* mean solar time.

The following table, giving the values of the equation at noon, taken from the *Nautical Almanac*, for a few dates, will suffice to show its variations throughout the year. The sign + is prefixed when it is to be added to apparent

time, — when it is to be subtracted. The dates of the maximum values are
included :—

				Mins.	Secs.						Mins.	Secs.
Jan.	1	.	.	+ 3	32	July	1	.	.	+ 3	28
Feb.	1	.	.	+ 13	43	„	27	.	.	+ 6	18
„	11	.	.	+ 14	26	Aug.	1	.	.	+ 6	9
March	1	.	.	+ 12	35	Sept.	1	.	.	+ 0	4
April	1	.	.	+ 4	4	„	2	.	.	— 0	14
„	15	.	.	+ 0	9	Oct.	1	.	.	— 10	10
„	16	.	.	— 0	5	Nov.	1	.	.	— 16	18
May	1	.	.	— 2	57	„	3	.	.	— 16	20
„	15	.	.	— 3	50	Dec.	1	.	.	— 11	0
June	1	.	.	— 2	30	„	24	.	.	— 0	30
„	14	.	.	— 0	7	„	25	.	.	0	0
„	15	.	.	+ 0	6	„	31	.	.	+ 2	58

The time shown by a sun-dial, being dependent on the true sun, is of course
apparent time. To obtain mean time from this, the equation must be added or
subtracted, in accordance with the directions given in the headings of the columns
in which it is published in many almanacs. The directions usually given are in
the words "clock before sun" and "clock after sun." In the former case the
equation must be added to sun-dial time, in the latter case it should be subtracted.
This gives *local* mean time ; if Greenwich mean time be required, the longitude in
time must be added if the place is west of Greenwich, or subtracted if east.

The difference between a mean solar day and a sidereal day will be more
easily understood if we imagine a fictitious or mean sun, as it is called, moving
uniformly in the heavens with the average motion of the real sun. If this sun and
a fixed star cross the meridian of a place at the same moment on any day, in
twenty-four hours of sidereal time the star will again be on the meridian, but the
sun will not yet have reached this position. During the day the earth has moved
about a degree in its orbit round the sun, causing the sun apparently to move the
same amount towards the east amongst the stars. Hence the meridian, which has
already reached the fixed star, requires a few minutes longer to reach the mean
sun. The sidereal day is thereafter shorter than the mean solar day. The exact
amount of this difference is 3 minutes 55·9 seconds of mean solar time, or 3 minutes
56·6 second of sidereal time. Hence—

A sidereal day   = 23 hours 56 minutes 4·1 seconds of mean solar time.
A mean solar day   = 24 hours 3 minutes 56·6 seconds of sidereal time.
1 sidereal hour   = 0 hours 59 minutes 50·2 seconds of mean time.
1 hour of mean time = 1 hour 0 minutes 9·9 seconds of sidereal time.

The great convenience of sidereal time in astronomical work arises from the
fact that the right ascension of the stars are measured from the first point of Aries,
as a starting-point, from west to east along the celestial equator. Right ascensions
may be expressed either in degrees, 360 to the whole equinoctial circle, or in time,
allowing 1 hour to 15 degrees. The latter method is now almost universally
adopted. If, therefore, the sidereal clock be started at 0 hours 0 minutes 0 seconds
at the moment when the first point of Aries is on the meridian, it will show 1 hour

o minutes o seconds when a star in 1 hour right ascension is on the meridian, and similarly it will show at any moment the right ascension of whatever celestial object or point of the celestial concave is on the meridian at the moment. In other words, the sidereal clock shows always the right ascension of the meridian. We thus arrive at the simplest and most accurate method of determining the true time or the error of the clock. It is the method used in all observatories. A convenient star is chosen, whose right ascension from frequent observation is well

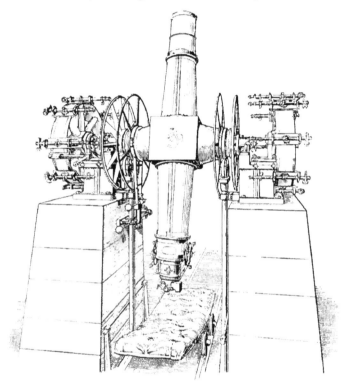

Fig. 6.

known. The moment, as shown by the clock, of its passage across the meridian is observed by means of a transit instrument (fig. 6), a telescope suitably fitted and mounted for the purpose. If, then, the time by the clock is the same as the known right ascension of the star, the clock is correct. If not, the difference is the error of the sidereal clock. It only remains, from the true sidereal time thus found, to determine the error of the mean time clock. To do this, the exact moment of coincident beats of the pendulums of the two clocks must be noted. We have then the true sidereal time at the instant of a particular second of the mean time clock. The nautical almanacs published annually by the British and other Governments provide the sidereal time at mean noon of the meridians to which the almanacs refer. We have then only to subtract this amount from the sidereal time of the coincidence noted and we have the interval of sidereal time elapsed at the moment of the coincidence since mean noon. We must now turn this into an interval of mean time, allowing 1 hour of sidereal to 0 hours 59 minutes 50·2 seconds of mean time. This interval of mean time elapsed since noon is what the mean time clock should show if correct, allowance being of course made for longitude if the observatory is not on the meridian for which the almanac has been computed. For example, suppose that at Edinburgh, on the 1st July 1908, the comparison of the clocks showed that 2 hours 52 minutes 54 seconds by the mean time clock was coincident with 9 hours 17 minutes 8 seconds by the sidereal, and that the sidereal clock was found to be 2·0 seconds slow by the latest observations, the true sidereal time would thus be 9 hours 17 minutes 10·0 seconds. From this subtract 6 hours 36 minutes 34·7 seconds, the sidereal time at Edinburgh mean noon, taken from the *Nautical Almanac*, and reduced to the longitude of Edinburgh, we have then 2 hours 40 minutes 35·3 seconds for the interval of sidereal time elapsed since Edinburgh mean noon. Now the equivalent of this interval in mean time can be found, from the value of 1 hour of sidereal time given above, by simple proportion, or it can be taken from a table specially prepared for the purpose. This comes out 2 hours 40 minutes 9·0 seconds, and this is what the clock ought to have shown if it were set to Edinburgh mean time. If, as is customary in Edinburgh, it is set to Greenwich mean time, we must add 12 minutes 44·2 seconds, the west longitude of Edinburgh. This gives 2 hours 52 minutes 53·2 seconds, the true Greenwich mean time of the coincidence of beats, when the clock time was 2 hours 52 minutes 54 seconds. Hence the clock was 0·8 second fast at the moment of comparison.

If the clocks in use at different parts of the country for the ordinary purposes of civil life were each set by a sun-dial corrected for the equation of time only, as explained above on p. 11, they would show local mean time, and would differ by the difference of longitude of the various sun-dials by which they were regulated. Thus a Glasgow clock would be 4½ minutes behind an Edinburgh clock, and a Liverpool clock would differ from a London one by 12¼ minutes. The facilities for rapid intercourse between one city and another provided by railways, and for the instantaneous interchange of ideas by telegraph, have long since rendered such a system highly inconvenient. To obviate this difficulty, in modern times all clocks in Great Britain have been set to Greenwich time. In France the time of the Paris meridian has been kept, and generally other nations have similarly adopted the time of the meridian of their principal observatory. This arrangement has great advantages for nations the east and west borders of whose territory do not differ very greatly in longitude, but is quite unsuitable in the case of such a country as the United States of America, where Washington and San Francisco, for instance, differ by fully three hours in longitude, and whose great railway lines run to so large an extent in an east and west direction. A movement in favour of an international system of standard time has, therefore, arisen of late years. This plan, which has already been adopted by the most important Governments of the world, starts from the meridian of Greenwich as the prime meridian for all countries, and divides the surface of the globe into sections covering 15° each, or 1 hour of longitude, in which the time of the central meridian of that section shall alone be kept. If it had been possible to carry out such an arrangement in its theoretical completeness, the section reaching from $7\frac{1}{2}°$ east to $7\frac{1}{2}°$ west of Greenwich would keep Greenwich time; the section stretching from $7\frac{1}{2}°$ west to $22\frac{1}{2}°$ west would be set 1 hour behind Greenwich, while the section $7\frac{1}{2}°$ to $22\frac{1}{2}°$ east would be 1 hour before Greenwich, and so on. Clocks all over the world would thus differ only in the hours shown, but would coincide in the minutes and seconds. The irregularities of the boundaries of countries and states would, of course, necessitate departures from the uniformity of such a desirable system, but these do not appear to be so great as to prevent its adoption, or even to introduce much practical inconvenience. Fig. 7 illustrates the application of this arrangement in the United States of America.

Nearly all European States have legalised standard time. Great Britain and

PACIFIC TIME   MOUNTAIN TIME   CENTRAL TIME   EASTERN TIME
8 hours behind Greenwich   7 hours behind Greenwich   6 hours behind Greenwich   5 hours behind Greenwich

FIG. 7.

Ireland, France, Belgium, Spain, and Portugal use West European time, which is the mean solar time of the meridian of Greenwich. In Italy, Switzerland, Germany, Luxembourg, Austria, Hungary, Serbia, Denmark, Norway, and Sweden the time used is Central European time, or that of the meridian $15°$ east—1 hour earlier than Greenwich time. The legal time in Rumania, Bulgaria, Turkey, Greece, Egypt, and in South Africa is Eastern European time—2 hours in advance of Greenwich. In India $5\frac{1}{2}$ hours, and in Burma $6\frac{1}{2}$ hours in advance of Greenwich have been adopted as the standard times for railway and other purposes. In Japan legal time is 9 hours in advance of Greenwich. In Australia three time sections have been arranged, which are 8, $9\frac{1}{2}$, and 10 hours respectively in advance of Greenwich. New Zealand time is $11\frac{1}{2}$ hours also in advance. Canada and the United States have legalised five sections—4, 5, 6, 7, and 8 hours behind Greenwich time. The advantages of this system for purposes of telegraphic communication, and for use on railways crossing large continents in an east and west direction, are easily recognisable.

The method of determining true sidereal time, and from it deducing true mean solar time, as practised in observatories, has been described above. Without attempting any detailed account of the methods of finding time at sea and by explorers, or describing the instrument chiefly employed, a few words may be said here to indicate how astronomical observations are made use of for this purpose, and to show how the longitude of a ship's place at sea may be obtained from it, combined with a knowledge of the time at Greenwich at the same moment, a result of incalculable value to a seafaring nation. Observations made at sea consist, for the greater part, of measures of the angle subtended at the eye by

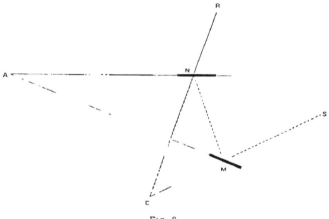

FIG. 8.

the distance between two heavenly bodies, such as a star and the moon's edge, or the altitude of the sun or a star above the horizon. The simplest and most convenient instrument for this purpose is the sextant, invented by Mr Hadley in 1731. It consists essentially of a frame, on which two mirrors are so mounted that the image of one of the objects seen after two reflections can be made to coincide in direction with the other object seen directly.

In fig. 8, M and N are the two mirrors, mounted at right angles to the plane of the paper, of which M can be made to rotate by means of the arm, M A. When M has been brought into the position shown, the image of an object in the direction S will reach the eye at E along the broken lines after two reflections, while the other object in the direction R is seen directly, crossing N just above the reflecting portion. It is a simple exercise in geometry to show that the angle at E is double that at A. The latter angle is measured by the movement of the arm, M A, necessary to bring the mirror, M, into the proper position to reflect the image of S to E. This is the principle involved in Hadley's sextant. The instrument being held in the hand during use, the observation

B

is not affected by the unsteadiness of the ship, as a similar observation with any conceivable form of telescope would certainly be.

The problem of determining the time at sea, as well as on land, depends on finding by some method the time when the sun or one of the brighter stars crosses the meridian of the place. We know that a heavenly body is at its greatest altitude above the horizon when it is on the meridian. If, then, we can observe the time when the highest altitude is attained, we have immediately our local time. The time of meridian altitude cannot, however, be observed directly with the sextant with much accuracy, because when close to the meridian the altitude increases very slowly till the meridian is reached, and then diminishes very slowly and therefore a large error in the time might be made. Instead of this, the method usually adopted is to observe the times when the altitude is the same at both sides of the meridian and at some considerable distance from it. In the case of a star the mean of these times gives the time when the star was on the meridian. If the chronometer were rated to show sidereal time, the time of the meridian passage so found would be the star's right ascension, as explained on page 13. If there were any difference between the time shown and the right ascension taken from the *Nautical Almanac*, this difference would be the error of the chronometer. The true sidereal time can be turned into local mean time, as already explained. Similar pairs of altitude observations of the sun may be used for this purpose, but in this the problem is somewhat complicated by the fact that the sun's declination alters sensibly during the five or six hours intervening between the two observations, and consequently the same altitude of the sun does not occur at equal distances at each side of the meridian. The necessary allowance to be made can, however, be calculated mathematically, and presents no very considerable difficulty. The time found by these observations of the sun would be the moment of apparent noon by chronometer. If the latter is rated to show mean solar time, the application of the equation of time would then give the instant of local mean noon.

Having obtained the mean solar time for the position of his ship, a further knowledge of the time at the same moment at some place of known longitude, such as Greenwich Observatory, would enable the sailor to find his own longitude, and, provided he also had observed the latitude, he could lay down the place of his ship on a chart, and shape his course in a direct line towards his destination, instead of sailing north or south into the latitude of the haven to which he was bound, and then "running down the port on the parallel." The time at Greenwich can be secured by several methods, but it will be sufficient to refer to two only— by chronometers and by the observation of lunar distances. All ocean-going vessels now carry with them one or more chronometers, which, previous to the beginning of the voyage, have been set to Greenwich time, or have had their errors carefully determined. In addition, the rate of increase or decrease of their errors must have been carefully examined at various temperatures. If their rates remained absolutely unchanged, chronometers might be relied upon for finding Greenwich time after applying the accumulated errors. It has been found, however, that the rate differs slightly when at sea from that determined when at rest on land. An astronomical method of finding Greenwich time is therefore necessary in order to check the going of a chronometer. This is provided by the "lunar distances" given for every third hour of Greenwich time in the pages of the *Nautical Almanac*. These consist of the angular distances of the centre of the moon from the centre of the sun, and from some of the brighter stars and planets, as these distances would appear if seen from the centre of the earth. Equipped with the *Almanac*, which is published three or four years in advance, the sailor measures with his sextant the distance between the moon and one of the objects named, and notes the time by his chronometer. He then has to clear his measure from the effects of parallax and refraction, thus reducing it to what it would have been if it had been observed from the centre of the earth. If the distance so reduced is found exactly given in the *Almanac*, then the hour named at the head of the page is the Greenwich mean time of the moment of the observation, and nothing further is necessary but to compare it with the local mean time to find the longitude desired. If, however, the exact angular distance measured is not found in the *Almanac*, but lies between two of the distances given there for intervals of three hours, the proper proportional part of the three hours must be calculated and allowed for. Easy rules for performing this operation are given in the *Almanac*. Great accuracy is necessary in the measurement of the lunar distances made use of in this method. The moon moves towards the

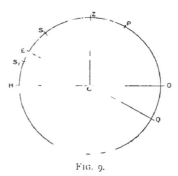

FIG. 9.

east in the sky at the rate of about 1 degree in 2 hours, or of 1 minute of arc in 2 minutes of time. Hence an error of 1 minute in the measure may lead to an error of 2 minutes of time in the longitude, or of about 30 miles at the equator. A seaman expert in the use of the sextant can usually determine his longitude with an error of much less than this. To the late Dr Maskelyne, Astronomer-Royal from 1765 to 1811, is due the credit of strongly advocating the use of lunar distances for finding Greenwich time at sea. He also recommended that the *Nautical Almanac* should be published for the purpose of facilitating its general adoption. The first annual volume appeared in 1767. Of late years, however, this method of determining the longitude at sea has fallen into disuse to such an extent, that the Lunar Distances have been omitted from the *Nautical Almanac*, seamen now preferring to depend on observations of the altitudes of stars, or of the moon and planets as the most convenient method of ascertaining the position at sea both in latitude and longitude.

The problem of finding the latitude at sea is much more simple than that of finding the longitude. We have defined the latitude of a place on the earth's surface as its angular distance from the equator measured by an arc of the meridian, or the angle at the earth's centre subtended by this arc. If, now, we draw a radius from the earth's centre to a point on its surface, and produce it upwards to the sky, it will reach the celestial concave in the point known as the zenith of the place. Hence the latitude of a place is evidently the angle between the zenith and the equinoctial measured along the celestial meridian. This fact at once suggests a simple means of finding the latitude by astronomical observation. If the place be in the northern hemisphere, and the sun's declination or distance from the equator also north, then the latitude can be found by adding the sun's declination to its meridian zenith distance. If the declination be south, we must subtract it from the zenith distance. The latter quantity can easily be measured with the instruments to be found in a fixed observatory, but at sea, where the sextant alone can be used, this cannot be done directly. Instead, the sun's meridian altitude or distance from the horizon must be taken, and by subtracting this from 90° the zenith distance is found.

If in the figure (fig. 9) the circle be the meridian of a place in the northern hemisphere, of which Z is the zenith, H O at right angles to Z C will be the rational horizon. If P be the north pole, and E Q perpendicular to P C the equator, then the arc Z E is the latitude of the place. If S be the sun on the meridian in north declination, Z E is equal to Z S, the sun's meridian zenith distance + S E, the sun's declination. Also, if S_1 be the sun on the meridian in south declination, $Z S_1 - S_1 E$ is equal to Z E. It will also be seen from the figure that the arc O P is equal to Z E, because if to each of these we add the arc P Z we get an arc of 90°. Hence O P also measures the latitude, which is therefore equal to the altitude of the pole above the north point of the horizon.

CHAPTER IV.

THE CORRECTIONS TO BE APPLIED TO ASTRONOMICAL OBSERVATIONS.

THE most important of the disturbing causes which affect the apparent position of heavenly bodies on the celestial concave, and which must be applied before observations of their places can be made use of for the advancement of the theory of their movements are Refraction, Aberration, Precession, Nutation, and Parallax.

Astronomical **Refraction** is the effect produced on the apparent position of a heavenly body by the passage, through the earth's atmosphere, of the rays by which it is seen. Light passing through a uniform medium is propagated in straight lines. When it passes from a rarer into a denser medium it is bent out of the straight line towards the perpendicular to the bounding surface across which it is passing. Thus, the ray by which a star, or any celestial object, is seen, travels in a straight line through the uniform ether pervading space, till it reaches the upper surface of the atmosphere. Here, unless the object is in the zenith, it is refracted or bent, as shown in Plate I., fig. 2, and more bent the more it advances into the lower and denser regions of the atmosphere, thus describing a curved path through the air. The Plate shows the true path of the ray from a star, and its apparent direction as affected by refraction. It also shows to the nearest half minute the amount of the correction for refraction at all altitudes above the horizon, ranging from nothing at the zenith to thirty-three minutes at the horizon. The amount of refraction near the horizon is subject to some uncertainty, owing to the variability of the conditions of pressure, temperature, and moisture, all of which affect refraction very largely in the lower strata of the atmosphere. Consequently astronomers confine their observations as much as possible to objects at some elevation above the horizon. The illustration shows the rapid increase of the amount of refraction as the lowest altitudes are approached. The object under observation is apparently visible in the direction in which the ray at last meets the eye, or along the tangent to the curved path of the ray. Hence, the effect of refraction is to increase the altitude of the star above the horizon. As the whole foundation of the theory of the movements of the heavenly bodies consists of accurate determinations of their places on the celestial sphere, such determination depending on observations with instruments, specially constructed for the purpose, it is necessary that all such observations must be carefully corrected for refraction. The construction of tables for supplying this correction is one of the difficulties the astronomer has to contend with, owing to the continual changes in the density of the atmosphere due to alterations of atmospheric pressure shown by the barometer, and of temperature.

To refraction is due the slightly oval shape of the sun or moon when seen in contact with the horizon. The amount of refraction increases very rapidly as the horizon is approached. Thus, on the horizon it is 34 minutes of arc, while at an altitude above the horizon equal to the sun's or moon's diameter it is less by nearly 5 minutes. Hence, when the sun or moon seems to be just touching the horizon its lower edge has really been elevated from below the horizon by 34 minutes, while its upper edge is raised only 29 minutes, resulting in a shortening of the vertical diameter while the horizontal diameter is unaffected. When seen in this position the sun or moon is really completely below the horizon. Twilight and dawn are also due to atmospheric refraction. By the effect of refraction in raising the sun above the horizon, the duration of daylight is increased about 4 minutes at sunrise and the same amount at sunset in the latitude of Edinburgh.

Aberration is another important correction which must be carefully attended to before astronomical observations can be made use of for any theoretical or practical purpose. It results from the progressive motion of light combined with the motion of the earth in its orbit. Light travels at the enormous rate of 186,000 miles in a second of time. Yet so great are the distances with which the science of astronomy has to deal, that even with this inconceivable velocity light takes 8 minutes 17 seconds to reach us from the sun. In this time the earth travels in its orbit through rather more than 20 seconds of arc, consequently the ray of light by which a point on the sun's surface is seen at any instant must have left the sun's surface at a moment when the earth was 20 seconds of arc behind its position at the instant of observation. Suppose, for a moment, the earth to be at rest. In such a case, in order to see a celestial object through a long tube, the tube would have to be pointed straight at the object. Further, suppose the light by which the object is seen to consist of a single ray. This ray on arrival at the upper end of the tube would travel straight down its centre to the eye of the observer in a direction parallel to its side. Now imagine the tube to be fixed in the above direction, but carried by the earth's motion through a distance equal to the radius of the tube, in the same time as the ray of light takes to travel down the tube. The ray would in this case strike against the edge of the tube, opposite to the direction of the earth's motion, and would not reach the eye of the observer. It is evident, therefore, that in order to see the object the tube must be inclined forward at the upper end in the direction of the earth's motion, and the angular amount of the inclination will depend on the ratio between the velocity of light and that of the earth in its orbit. A simple illustration of the phenomenon of aberration is shown in fig. 5, Plate I. The boat is passing rapidly in front of the battery and is pierced by a cannon ball. The hole by which the ball entered the boat would not be exactly opposite, but somewhat forward of that by which it passed out, and the direction of the line joining the centres of the two holes would not point to the gun but somewhat in advance of it. The general effect of aberration is to make a star appear to be somewhat in advance of its true place in the direction of the earth's movement in its orbit at the moment of observation. Thus in the course of the year the star appears to describe a small ellipse in the heavens about its true place. This effect of aberration is illustrated in fig. 4, Plate I. The discovery of this remarkable phenomenon is due to Bradley, Astronomer-Royal from 1742 to 1762.

The **Precession** of the Equinoxes is a slow retrogression of the equinoctial point, or intersection of the equator and the ecliptic, along the latter circle. In consequence of this backward movement of the equator along the ecliptic, the earth arrives each year at the equinoxes earlier than it would if there were no such retrogression. The equinoctial point, called the "first point of Aries," is the zero or starting point for right ascensions reckoned along the equator, and for longitude on the ecliptic. Owing to precession, Aries and all the signs of the Zodiac have shifted backwards with reference to the stars, though still retaining the names of the constellations with which they at one time coincided in position. The retrogression amounts to 50·1 seconds of arc in the year, so that a complete revolution through all the signs of Zodiac would occupy 25,868 years. It is due to a slow conical motion of the direction of the earth's axis around the pole of the ecliptic, which is itself the result of the attraction of the sun and moon on the protuberant matter at the earth's equator, combined with the centrifugal force resulting from the rotation of this equatorial belt. The figure of the earth is not a true sphere or globe, but a spheroid—that is to say, a figure nearly a sphere, but having its polar diameter shorter than its equatorial diameter. The attraction of the sun or moon is greater on that part of the equatorial belt nearest to these bodies than on the portion farthest away from them, thus producing a tendency to a change in the plane of the equator, and a consequent rotation of the axis about its mean position somewhat similar to that of a spinning-top. The attraction of the sun tends to pull the plane of the equator into the plane of the ecliptic, while that of the moon tends to pull it into that of the lunar orbit. The phenomenon of precession may be profitably studied experimentally with the help of a good-sized spinning-top or gyroscope. Experiments which the reader can easily perform for himself will help to explain some of the difficulties of the question.

The longitudes of all fixed stars vary by the whole amount of precession 50·1″ per annum, while the latitude is unaffected. Right ascensions and declinations also alter from year to year, but the amount of the corrections varies with the positions of the stars in the celestial sphere. The precession of the equinoxes was first discovered by Hipparchus.

Nutation may·be considered as a modification of precession, and was discovered by Bradley, who was also the discoverer of aberration. It is due chiefly to a change in the position of the moon's nodes, the points at which its orbit intersects the ecliptic. The earth's axis, instead of describing a circle about the pole of the ecliptic, as it would do if it were influenced alone by precession, constantly tends to describe a small ellipse about its place in that circle. The result of the combination of the two motions is a wavy curved line, the point where the earth's axis cuts the sky being sometimes nearer the pole of the ecliptic, sometimes farther from it than its mean position by about 9 seconds of arc.

Parallax of a heavenly body is illustrated in fig. 3 of Plate 1. In its general sense parallax signifies the change of apparent position of an object, due to change of position of the observer. Astronomically it refers to the correction to be applied to the apparent position of a heavenly body as seen from any point of the earth's surface, to reduce it to what its position would have been if viewed from the earth's centre. In the figure referred to above O is the position of the observer, B the moon on the horizon, and the angle at B subtended by the earth's radius, A O, is the moon's horizontal parallax. The moon is shown in three other positions, and for each of these the angle subtended by the radius is the parallax. It is clear from the illustration that the parallax is a maximum at the horizon, and vanishes altogether at the zenith. In the latter case the object is seen in the same direction whether viewed from O or from the earth's centre. By this correction, which is known as *diurnal* parallax, all observations are referred to the centre of the earth, being the only point of reference common to all observers. It will readily be seen on considering the parallax of the objects G and H, shown in the figure, that the nearer the object to the earth the greater is its parallax. Hence this correction is greatest in the case of the moon, amounting to from 61 to 54 minutes of arc on the horizon. The horizontal parallaxes of the sun and planets are smaller, but still appreciable, that of the sun being 8·80 seconds of arc. The radius of the earth being infinitely small when compared with the distances of the stars, these bodies are not affected by parallax in the sense in which we have been speaking. A very small number of the stars, however, have been found to be affected by parallax referred to the radius of the earth's orbit. The mean distance of the earth from the sun is 92,897,000 miles. This distance has been shown to subtend an angle of about three-quarters of a second of arc at the star α Centauri, and of nearly a third of a second at 61 Cygni. A few other stars have been found affected by small parallaxes, including the bright stars Sirius, Procyon, and Altair. These small angles affect the position of these stars at different times of the year, and the correction is known as *annual* parallax to distinguish it from *diurnal* parallax.

CHAPTER V.

DAY AND NIGHT—SEASONS.

THE phenomenon of the diurnal revolution of the celestial bodies round the poles of the heavens, which has been already referred to in Chapter I., may be explained by one of two causes—either the earth is at rest, and the sun, planets, and stars revolve round it as a centre from east to west, or else the earth rotates on an axis from west to east, and the diurnal revolution of the sky is only apparent, not real. The latter explanation will be at once accepted as the more natural one when we reflect on the different distances of the various bodies from the earth, the moon being much nearer to us than the sun, and the latter much nearer than the stars. The varying diameters of the planets also indicate great changes in their respective distances from the earth at different times. It is indeed difficult to conceive how so many bodies of different sizes, and at such varied and changing distances, could possibly be actuated in such a manner as to make them all revolve about a common centre. The simplicity of nature compels us to accept the earth's rotation on its axis as true. The matter is, however, not without practical proof. If a stone be let fall from the top of a high tower it will fall slightly to the east of the foot, owing to the greater velocity of rotation of the top than of the foot of the tower. A more satisfactory proof, however, is afforded by Foucault's pendulum experiments made in 1851. If a pendulum be suspended from a fixed point of support and made to vibrate in any plane, it will continue to vibrate in the same plane even though it be connected with the point of support by a spindle to which a motion of rotation is communicated. A complete explanation of the manner in which M. Foucault made use of this remarkable law of pendulum vibration to demonstrate the earth's rotation on its axis must be sought for by the reader in more advanced text-books of Astronomy. Here it is sufficient to say that if such a pendulum were suspended at the pole, an observer, unconscious of his own motion with the earth, would see an *apparent* revolution of the pendulum plane in 23 hours 56 minutes 4 seconds. In fact we know the pendulum plane cannot revolve, and the only possible explanation of its apparent revolution is that the earth has rotated beneath it in the time stated. Again, if the pendulum were set up at the equator, the earth would carry the spectator, the pendulum, its point of support and plane of vibration, in the same direction, with no change of position with respect to one another, and there would be here no such apparent motion of the pendulum plane as would be seen at the pole. It is of course impossible to suspend a pendulum at the pole of the earth, but experiments have been made at several places in different latitudes, all giving results from which the hourly apparent motion of the pendulum plane could be deduced, and the time of the earth's rotation on its axis computed. The results at the various places agree in giving values for the time of rotation as near to the true amount, 23 hours 56 minutes 4 seconds, as could be expected from experiments of a somewhat difficult nature.

Fig. 1, Plate II, illustrates the phenomenon of day and night, the most obvious result of the earth's rotation. The sun is shown illuminating that hemisphere of the earth which is turned towards it, every point of which will enjoy daylight, while the rotation is causing the sun to traverse its apparent path across the sky from its rising in the east to setting in the west.

If the axis upon which the earth performs its daily rotation had been perpendicular to the plane of the orbit round the sun, the sun would have been constantly, all day and all the year round, vertical to some point or other of the equator, and never vertical at any other part of the earth's surface. A few moments careful consideration of the figure will make it clear that in such a case day and night would have been equal all the world over, and each would have been of twelve hours duration. As a consequence of this equality of day and night all the year round, places in the same latitude would have the same invariable climate, and the vicissitudes of the seasons would have been unknown, so far as these depend on the sun's influence alone.

The earth's axis is, however, so inclined that the plane of the equator makes an angle of about $23\frac{1}{2}°$ with the plane of the orbit. From this simple fact the variation in the length of the day at different times of the year and in different latitudes at once follows, and the existence of this angle of inclination, known as the obliquity of the ecliptic, secures to the earth's inhabitants the succession of the seasons—spring time and harvest, summer and winter. Fig. 1, Plate II., shows how the obliquity of the ecliptic affects the length of the day. It will be seen that the position illustrated is that of winter in the northern hemisphere. The South Pole leans towards the sun, and the parallels of latitude are shown partly enlightened, partly in darkness. Just south of the equator the enlightened part of the parallel is slightly longer than the unenlightened, and here the day is slightly longer than the night, the sun rising a little before 6 A.M. local time and setting a little after 6 P.M. As we go towards the South Pole, the part of each parallel in the enlightened hemisphere is greater in proportion to the part in the dark hemisphere the nearer we get to the Pole, and the day more and more exceeds the night in length, the sun rising at a longer interval before 6 A.M., and setting longer after 6 P.M. We at last reach a parallel of latitude which is wholly within the enlightened hemisphere, where there is no night at the season of the year which the figure represents. Supposing this season to be exactly midsummer of the southern hemisphere, midwinter in the northern, we would reach this parallel at $23\frac{1}{2}°$ from the South Pole, or in $66\frac{1}{2}°$ of south latitude. This parallel is known as the Antarctic Circle. The sun is then vertical at the latitude parallel $23\frac{1}{2}°$ south of the equator, known as the Tropic of Capricorn, because the sun at this date, 22nd December, enters the sign of the Zodiac of that name. At midsummer of the northern hemisphere, 22nd June, the sun is vertical at noon over the latitude parallel $23\frac{1}{2}°$ north of the equator, known as the Tropic of Cancer. There is at this date no night from the North Pole to the Arctic Circle, $66\frac{1}{2}°$ north.

In latitudes farther north than $66\frac{1}{2}°$ the sun remains above the horizon for a lengthened period before and after midsummer day; at $66\frac{1}{2}°$ for twenty-four hours, at $67\frac{1}{2}°$ for one month, at $78°$ for about four months, and at the Pole for six months. The Arctic night lasts for similar intervals, relieved, however, by the long dawn and twilight of high latitudes, and by the presence of the moon for a number of days in succession about the time of full phase. During the whole Arctic night the sun, and consequently the new moon, are in south declination ; but the full moon, being in the part of the sky opposite to the sun, will be in north declination, and therefore continuously above the horizon of a great part of the Arctic Circle. The December and January moons are visible inside the Arctic Circle for nearly the whole time between first and last quarters. Auroras also play a part in mitigating the dreariness of the Arctic night.

In fig. 2, Plate II., are shown the earth's orbit round the sun and the inclination of the axis of rotation, or line joining the North and South Poles, with reference to the sun and the plane of the orbit, at the four dates :—

March 21	.	.	.	Spring Equinox.
June 22 .	.	.	.	Summer Solstice.
September 23	.	.	.	Autumnal Equinox.
December 22	.	.	.	Winter Solstice.

The signs of the Zodiac are shown by their symbols, for which *see* p. 9, and the months corresponding thereto are named on the outer ellipse. Thus, at the spring equinox, the earth as seen from the sun enters the sign Libra, and consequently the sun is found entering the opposite sign Aries. In this relative position of earth and sun, the intersection of the equator and ecliptic is on the line joining the centres of the sun and earth, the noonday sun is vertically over the equator, and day and night are equal all over the world.

It will be remarked at once, on inspection of the illustration, that throughout the whole of the earth's journey round the sun, the direction of which is indicated by the arrows, the successive positions of the axis of rotation are all parallel to one another. As the earth advances in its orbit during the months of April, May, and June, the sun passes through the signs of Aries, Taurus, and Gemini in succession, and the North Pole becomes more and more inclined towards the sun, and that luminary appears at noon vertical over a parallel of latitude farther and farther north of the equator. During this season—spring—the day continues to increase in length in the northern hemisphere till the sun reaches the beginning of the sign Cancer, and is vertical over the tropic of that name. This is the moment of the summer solstice, about 22nd June, when the sun reaches its greatest elevation in the northern hemisphere, when the days are longest, and the sun's heat reaches the surface of the earth more nearly vertical than at any other time of the year in latitudes north of the Tropic of Cancer. At the same time it is midwinter in the southern hemisphere, and the sun's rays reach the earth in latitudes south of Capricorn then most obliquely, and so exercise their minimum influence.

In the three following months, July, August, and September, while the sun is passing through the signs Cancer, Leo, and Virgo, the North Pole is gradually turning away from the sun, and the sun descends towards the equator. If we were to observe its altitude above the horizon each day at noon, or when it is due south, we would find it growing less and less until on the 23rd September, when at the beginning of the sign Libra, it has reached the celestial equator, and day has once more become equal to night.

During October, November, and December the sun's altitude at noon continues to decrease. It is now passing through the signs Libra, Scorpio, and Sagittarius, and about the 22nd December, when entering the sign of Capricornus, or at the winter solstice, its altitude is least in the northern hemisphere. We have at this season our shortest days and longest nights, and the sun's rays reach this hemisphere more obliquely than at any other time of the year. From this date the sun's elevation at noon begins to increase as it passes, in January, February, and March, through the signs Capricornus, Aquarius, and Pisces. On 21st March the sun again reaches the first point of Aries, and is vertical over the equator.

The seasonal alternations of heat and cold are thus evidently brought about by two causes—the varying proportion of the twenty-four hours during which the sun is above the horizon at different seasons, and the equally varying obliquity with which the sun's rays reach the earth's surface. The annexed figure conveys an idea of the angles at which the sun's rays reach the latitude of Edinburgh in midsummer and in midwinter :—

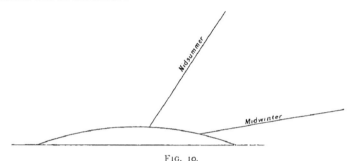

FIG. 10.

The four quarters into which the year is divided by the sun's entry into the signs Aries, Cancer, Libra, and Capricornus are not of precisely equal lengths owing to the earth's orbit not being exactly a circle, but an ellipse, with the sun in one of the foci. (This fact is not shown in the illustration to which we have been referring). The earth is nearest to the sun, or at perihelion, in the beginning of January, and farthest from it, or at aphelion, in July. In accordance with the laws of elliptic motion, the smaller the distance between these two bodies the faster do we travel in our orbit. Hence it results that the winter half of the year is shorter than the summer for the northern hemisphere.

In 1907-1908 the successive quarters of the year were of the following lengths :—

Spring—From Vernal Equinox to Summer Solstice, 92 days 19 hours 50 minutes.

Summer—From Summer Solstice to Autumnal Equinox, 93 days 14 hours 46 minutes.

Autumn—From Autumnal Equinox to Winter Solstice, 89 days 18 hours 43 minutes.

Winter—From Winter Solstice to Spring Equinox, 89 days 0 hours 35 minutes.

Hence the summer half of the year consisted of 186 days 10 hours 36 minutes, and the winter half of 178 days 19 hours 18 minutes; the winter was therefore the shorter by 7 days 15 hours 18 minutes.

CHAPTER VI.

APPARENT MOVEMENTS OF THE PLANETS.

PLATE VII. is intended to give a general idea of the arrangement of the planetary or solar system, the orbits of all the planets being shown, from Mercury, the nearest to the sun, to Neptune, the outermost, and to illustrate the position which the earth's orbit occupies with reference to the orbits of the other planets.

It will be noticed that the orbits of Mercury and Venus lie wholly within that of the earth, or nearer to the sun. They are hence called *inferior* planets, the name *superior* being applied to those planets whose orbits lie farther from the sun than that of the earth.

The inferior planets, owing to their position inside the orbit of the earth, never increase their angular distance from the sun beyond a certain amount.

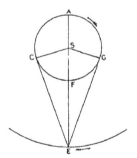

FIG. 11.

Sometimes they appear a little to the east of the sun, and set after it; when in this position relatively to the sun they are known as evening stars. At other times they are west of the sun, and consequently rise before it, and are called morning stars. In the course of their revolutions the inferior planets present phases like the moon, due to their varying positions relatively to the sun and earth.

In the annexed figure let A C F G represent the orbit of Mercury or Venus, and suppose for the moment that the earth is at rest at the point E in its orbit. At the points F and A the planet is in the same direction from the earth as the sun is, and is said to be in conjunction with the sun, F being for distinction called inferior conjunction, and A superior conjunction.

At F the whole of the enlightened hemisphere of the planet is turned away from the earth, and it is for a time invisible. As it moves along its orbit from F to G it gradually turns more of its enlightened side to the earth, and is seen as a crescent, at first very thin, but widening till it appears like a half moon at G. From G to A more than half of the bright side is turned towards us, and the planet assumes the gibbous form, which goes on increasing till at A the whole of the enlightened side is turned towards us.

At this point the planet is again for some time invisible owing to its proximity to the sun's rays. In its path from A through C to F a similar succession of phases takes place, but in reversed order. The phases of an inferior planet are illustrated in fig. 7, Plate I.

At the points C and G (fig. 11) at which the line E C is at right angles to C S and E G to G S, when, as we have seen, the half-moon phases take place, the planet's angular distance from the sun as seen from the earth is the greatest—in other words, its greatest elongation east or west of the sun is when it is at one of these points, and it then sets at the longest interval after the sun or rises at the longest before it In the foregoing explanation we have supposed the orbits of Mercury and Venus to be circular and the earth at rest. In such a case the planets would repeat each of their various phases in succession after a complete revolution in their respective orbits and their greatest elongations would be always of the same angular amount.

As, however, their orbits as well as that of the earth are elliptical and not circular, considerable modifications of the above explanation must be made. As shown by the arrows in Plate VII. the earth moves in its orbit in the same direction as Venus and Mercury move in theirs, namely, in the direction opposite to that of the hands of a watch ; Venus, however, makes a complete revolution in about 225 days, Mercury in about 88 days, whereas the earth takes $365\frac{1}{4}$ days to complete its orbit. Hence both the inferior planets move more rapidly in their orbits than the earth does. After the point where one of these planets, say Venus, is between the earth and the sun, or in inferior conjunction with the sun, has been passed, Venus gets rapidly ahead of the earth and arrives at the same point of its orbit in 225 days. But the earth by this time has moved more than half way round its orbit, and Venus, therefore, has to follow up and overtake the earth before inferior conjunction can again take place. A similar consideration holds with reference to the other phases—superior conjunction, greatest elongation, etc. Hence the complete cycle of the planet's phases, or its synodical revolution, is only complete after 584 days in the case of Venus, and 116 in the case of Mercury ; periods for both much longer than their respective sidereal revolutions. The ellipticity of the orbits has the further effect of varying the angular distance of Venus or Mercury from the sun at the moments of their greatest east and west elongations.

Thus in 1907, according to the *Nautical Almanac*, the greatest elongations of Mercury east of the sun were, on 2nd March 18°, on 27th June 25°, and on 23rd October 24°. Greatest east and west elongations of Venus occurred on 8th February 1907, 47° west, and on 26th April 1908, $45\frac{1}{2}$° east. Mercury's greatest elongations vary from 16° to 29° ; those of Venus from 45° to 48°.

In consequence of the great difference in the distances separating the earth from either of the inner planets at inferior conjunction and at superior conjunction, the apparent sizes of these planets also vary greatly. They appear of largest diameter when crescents, just before or after inferior conjunction, and smallest when, near superior conjunction, they are sufficiently removed from the sun's rays to be visible. When Venus has passed inferior conjunction its crescent gradually increases in breadth, and from this cause its brightness becomes greater and greater every day. At the same time, however, its increasing distance from the earth and lessening apparent diameter reduce the apparent size and brightness, as illustrated in fig. 7, Plate I. The brightness of the planet Venus thus depends on two circumstances—phase and distance from the earth. The question then arises, in what part of its orbit does Venus shine with greatest brightness? Not when the whole disc is illuminated at superior conjunction, because it is then farthest from the earth, nor yet at inferior conjunction, because when seen near this point it appears as a very thin crescent. There must, therefore, be some intermediate point between the superior and inferior conjunctions at which Venus shines most brightly. This position of greatest brilliancy is found to correspond to those points of its orbit at which Venus arrives about thirty-five days before greatest elongation west, and the same number of days after greatest elongation east. Thus in 1907 Venus shone with greatest brilliancy as a morning star on

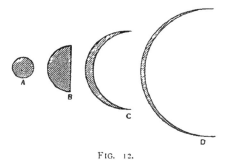

FIG. 12.

Showing the comparative sizes of Venus when at (A) superior conjunction ; (B) greatest elongation ; (C) greatest brilliancy ; and (D) near inferior conjunction.

the 4th January, and the greatest elongation west occurred on the 9th February. As an evening star it was at greatest elongation east on the 26th April 1908, and the greatest brilliancy followed on the 29th May. These are of course the theoretical positions of greatest brilliancy ; as a matter of fact Venus, when near these two positions, can be seen with the naked eye in broad daylight for several weeks in succession.

An interesting feature in the apparent movement of the planets is that they sometimes appear to change the direction of their path among the stars, a circumstance which suggested to the Greeks the name planets, or wanderers. For an inferior planet this will be readily understood from a consideration of the figure on p. 29. Suppose Venus to have just passed superior conjunction at A, it is then moving farther and farther to the east of the sun, and its motion among the stars, into whose apparent neighbourhood it is projected along the line of sight from the earth, is also towards the east ; at the same time, the earth's motion being in the opposite direction round our orbit causes Venus to move apparently still more towards the east. Hence in all that portion of its orbit about superior conjunction Venus moves towards the east among the stars. Again, at inferior conjunction, about the point F, the motion of Venus is to the west of the sun, and the earth's motion is in the same direction ; but that of Venus is more rapid than the earth's, and hence it appears to move to the west among the stars, or in an opposite direction to its path at superior conjunction. When the apparent motion of a planet is from west to east, or in the direction of the Zodiacal signs in the order in which the sun traverses them, it is said to be *direct*, when from east to west it is known as *retrograde*.

The motion of the planets Venus and Mercury, being direct at superior conjunction and retrograde at inferior conjunction, it follows that there must be two points between at which it is neither direct or retrograde ; where, in fact, the planet has no apparent motion among the stars. These are called the planets' stationary points, and are for Venus about forty to fifty days after greatest elongation east, and before greatest elongation west.

In the case of the superior planets a similar retrograde motion takes place when the planet is in opposition, that is, when the earth is between the planet and

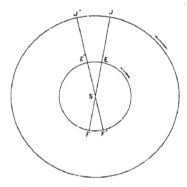

FIG. 13.

the sun. Thus in the figure let J be the position of a superior planet in opposition, the earth being then at E, the real motions of the planet and the earth are in the same direction, but the earth being closer to the sun moves at a greater speed, consequently the superior planet falls behind and apparently moves in the contrary or retrograde direction. On the other hand, when the planet is in conjunction, that is, as seen from the earth in the same direction as the sun, the planet at J, and the earth at F in the figure, the real movements are in opposite directions, and combined they give the planet an apparent motion towards the east.

Hence there will be at two dates, intermediate between conjunction and opposition, stationary points in a superior planet's apparent motion. At the time of conjunction of a superior planet, it is evident that the planet will rise and set nearly at the same time as the sun, and will be due south along with the sun about noon. At the time of opposition to the sun, on the other hand, the planet will be due south about midnight. At this time the planet is also nearer to the earth than it is at conjunction by the whole diameter of the earth's orbit. Hence a superior planet is best seen and observed about the time of opposition. The best time for observing an inferior planet is evidently at its greatest elongations east as an evening star, and west as a morning star. Mercury, indeed, whose greatest elongation, as we have seen, is never more than 29°, should be looked for within a few days of its most favourable positions.

The synodical period of the superior planets will be understood after precisely the same considerations as hold for the inferior planets, except that in their case the earth is the more rapidly moving body, being nearer the sun. It is important to distinguish clearly between a planet's sidereal period and its synodical period. The former is the time in which a planet makes a complete revolution round the sun, as referred to the stars, or the time which elapses between its appearance in any position amongst the stars, as seen from the sun, and its reappearance in the same position. The synodical period is the interval which elapses between two successive similar positions of the planet with respect to the earth and sun, such as two successive oppositions.

It is evident that the synodical period of a superior planet must be greater than the earth's sidereal revolution. In the case of Mars it will exceed this amount most largely, because Mars being the next planet farther from the sun than the earth, its rate of motion approaches more nearly that of the earth than do the motions of the planets still farther from the sun. Hence the earth after reaching the position it held at the last opposition of Mars, takes more time to make up for the motion of that planet, and bring it again into opposition, than it does to make up on the more slowly moving outer planets.

The following table shows the sidereal revolutions of the planets, and their synodical periods :—

				Sidereal.	Synodical.
MERCURY	.	.	.	88 days	116 days
VENUS .	.	.	.	225 ,,	583 ,,
EARTH .	.	.	.	365¼ ,,	—
MARS .	.	.	.	1 year 322 ,,	780 ,,
JUPITER	.	.	.	11 years 315 ,,	399 ,,
SATURN	.	.	.	29 ,, 167 ,,	378 ,,
URANUS	.	.	.	84 ,, 7 ,,	370 ,,
NEPTUNE	.	.	.	164 ,, 280 ,,	368 ,,

The complete cycle of the phases, and of the changes of the apparent motion of a planet, takes place in its synodical revolution. Hitherto we have supposed, for the sake of simplicity, that the planets revolve round the sun in orbits whose planes coincide with that of the earth's orbit. This, however, is not the case. All the greater planets revolve in orbits whose planes are slightly inclined to the ecliptic, that of Mercury having the greatest inclination, about 7°, Venus nearly 3½°, Saturn 2½°, and the others all less than 2°. On the other hand, the orbits of the minor planets are in many instances inclined to the ecliptic at much greater angles.

C

CHAPTER VII.

REAL MOVEMENTS OF THE PLANETS.

IN the last chapter attention was drawn to the apparent movements of the planets as seen projected on the sky in the line of sight, we now come to consider their real movements in their orbits round the sun, the real motions which, combined with the earth's motion, produce the apparent movement amongst the stars. After due allowance is made for the effect of the earth's motion on the apparent motion of a planet, it is found that there still remain certain peculiarities in the planet's movement. When the planet arrives at a certain part of the sky its velocity is invariably most rapid, and when seen in the opposite position of the sky its velocity is least rapid. Between these extremes the velocity varies, gradually increasing from the least to the greatest value. The relative distance of the planet from the sun is further found to be greatest when the velocity is least, and *vice versa*. No satisfactory explanation of these phenomena was forthcoming till the immortal Kepler demonstrated that the orbit of a planet, or its path round the sun, was the oval curve known as an ellipse. He further demonstrated the laws by which the varying velocities of a planet in its orbit are regulated, and showed how the periodic times, or complete revolutions of all the planets of the solar system, are related to each other, and depend on the mean distances of the planets from the sun. The discoveries of this famous astronomer are embodied in three propositions, universally known as Kepler's laws. They are (1) the planets revolve round the sun in ellipses, having the sun in one of the foci ; (2) the imaginary line joining the centre of the sun to the centre of the planet sweeps over equal areas in equal times ; (3) the squares of the periodic times are proportional to the cubes of the semi-major axes.

An ellipse may be constructed by the following simple method. Fasten two drawing-pins in a piece of cardboard, in such a way that a loop of thin thread may be passed under their heads. With the point of a pencil stretch the string quite tight, so as to form a triangle, of which one side is that part of the thread from the shank of one pin to the other, and the two other sides are the thread from the pencil point to each of the pins. Draw the point of the pencil along the cardboard, taking care to keep the thread always stretched. The resulting curve will be an ellipse.

In the figure F and G are the heads of the pins, and A F G A the thread. When the pencil point is at A let the pencil be moved from A to B, and on to C, and from C through D to E. and on to A. It is clear from the construction that the lines A F and A G together are equal to B F and B G together, or to C F and C G. In fact, the two lines drawn from any point on the ellipse to F and G, which are called the *foci*, are together equal to the two similarly drawn from any other point in the curve. This is the fundamental property of the ellipse. It is again evident that the nearer the points F and G are to one another, the more nearly will the curve approach in form to a circle, and when the points actually coincide the resulting curve is a circle. Also the longer the loop of thread, the nearer will the ellipse be in form to a circle. These two facts combined constitute what is called by mathematicians the *eccentricity* of the ellipse ; or rather, they enable a measure of the eccentricity to be found, by which the form of one ellipse can be compared with that of another. It is .evident from the method of construction that C F is equal to E G, therefore C E, called the major axis, is equal to C F and C G together, or to the two lines drawn from any point on the ellipse, and if H be the centre of the ellipse, C H, the semi-axis major, will be half that amount. The eccentricity is expressed numerically by the ratio of F G to C E, or the ratio of the distance between the foci to the axis major. Such is the curve in which the planets revolve round the sun, having, in accordance with Kepler's first law, the sun in one of the foci. Let F in the figure be the focus in which the sun is situated When the planet is at C it is in *perihelion*, or nearest the sun, when at E it is in *aphelion*, or away from the sun. C F is

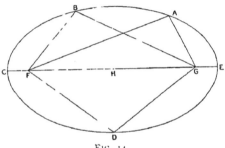

Fig. 14.

called the perihelion distance, E F the aphelion distance. The average of all the distances of the planet from the sun through a complete revolution is called the *mean distance*.

It has been already stated that the planets revolve about the sun in orbits whose planes do not coincide with the ecliptic, or plane of the earth's orbit As each of the orbits has the sun in one of its foci, it follows that every planet's orbit must intersect the plane of the earth's orbit in two points at opposite sides of the sun, half of a planet's orbit lying towards the north side of the ecliptic and half towards the south. These points are called the *nodes* of the planet's orbit. That one at which the planet passes from the south to the north side of the ecliptic is called the *ascending node*, and the one at which it returns from the north to the south side is called the *descending node*. When a planet is at either of these nodes it is also then in the plane of the ecliptic. In any other position in its orbit it is either north of the ecliptic or south of it. If, when either of the planets Mercury or Venus is at or close to one of the nodes, it is also in inferior conjunction with the sun, that is, passing between the earth and the sun, it will be projected on the sun's disc, and a transit of the planet across the sun will take place. (These transits will be referred to later.) If at inferior conjunction either of these planets is at a distance from its nodes, no such transit will take place, but the planet will pass either above or below the sun, but so close as to be lost to sight in the sun's rays. The following particulars with reference to the orbit of a planet must be known before its place can be predicted for a future date. They are called the elements of the orbits.

(1) The semi-major axis of the orbit, or mean distance of the planet from the sun.
(2) The eccentricity of the orbit.
(3) The longitude of the perihelion.
(4) The inclination of its orbit to the ecliptic.
(5) The longitude of the ascending node.
(6) The mean longitude of the planet, corresponding to a given date.

The first two elements define the magnitude of the orbit, as compared with other orbits in the solar system, and the form of the ellipse, the third fixes the position of the axis major in the plane of the orbit. Elements (4) and (5) fix the position of the orbit with reference to the ecliptic. The sixth element fixes the place of a planet in its orbit at a particular date. When these six elements have been determined by computation from observation of a planet, it is possible by the application of Kepler's laws to find its place in the sky at any past or future date. The elements, however, vary slightly and very slowly owing to perturbations due to the attractive influence of the planets on one another. It is necessary, therefore, in stating the elements to give the dates to which they correspond. Another cause of their variation is due to the slow movement of the "first point of Aries" arising from the precession of the equinoxes.

The following elements of the eight greater planets are taken from the *Annales de l'Observatoire de Paris*, and correspond to the date 1st January 1850:—

Name.	Semi-axis Major.	Eccentricity.	Longitude of Perihelion.	Inclination of Orbit to Ecliptic.	Longitude of Ascending Nodes.	Mean Longitude Jan. 1, 1850.
☿ MERCURY	0·3871	0·2056	75°·7′	7°·0′	46°·33′	327°·15′
♀ VENUS .	0·7233	0·0068	129°·27′	3°·24′	75°·20′	245°·33′
⊕ EARTH .	1·0000	0·0168	100°·22′	—	—	100°·47′
♂ MARS .	1·5237	0·0933	333°·18′	1°·51′	48°·24′	83°·41′
♃ JUPITER .	5·2028	0·0483	11°·55′	1°·19′	98°·56′	160°·1′
♄ SATURN .	9·5389	0·0561	90°·7′	2°·30′	112°·21′	14°·52′
♅ URANUS .	19·1833	0·0463	170°·50′	0°·46′	73°·14′	29°·18′
♆ NEPTUNE	30·0551	0·0090	46°·0′	1°·47′	130°·6′	334°·33′

From even a cursory examination of the foregoing table, in which the planets are placed in the order of increasing distance from the sun, it will be seen that the orbit of Mercury is peculiar in two respects; first, the inclination to the ecliptic is greater than that of any other of the eight major planets, and, secondly, its eccentricity is also the greatest—in other words, its orbit differs from a circle more than any of the others do. The orbit of Venus, the planet next in order of distance from the sun, has the least eccentricity, or differs but slightly from a circle, while the orbit with the smallest inclination to the ecliptic is that of Uranus. Plate VII. shows the position of the orbits of the groups of small planets, or asteroids, as they were called by Sir William Herschel, lying between the orbits of Mars and Jupiter.

When Kepler was studying the laws of planetary motion he was much struck, when considering the relative distances of the orbits from one another, by the curious fact that a gap existed between the orbits of Mars and Jupiter disproportionately great as compared with the intervals between the other orbits.

Many attempts have been made to discover a simple law or relationship between the distances of the various planets from the sun. It was not till 1772 previous to the discovery of Uranus and Neptune, that Bode published an approximate law, which may be stated as follows. If we take the eight numbers—0, 3, 6, 12, 24, 48, 96, 192, each of which, except the first, is half the following one; if to each of those we add 4, we have the following series of numbers—4, 7, 10, 16, 28, 52, 100, 196, which, with a close degree of approximation, give the proportions existing between the mean distances of the planets from the sun. Thus, if 10 represents the distance of the earth from the sun, 4 would be the distance of Mercury, 7 that of Venus, 16 that of Mars, 52 that of Jupiter, and 100 that of Saturn. The following table, in which Uranus has been included, shows how closely the approximate distances derived from this empiric law agree with the true distances.

	Real Distance.	According to Bode's Law.
MERCURY	3·9	4·0
VENUS . . .	7·2	7·0
EARTH	10·0	10·0
MARS	15·2	16·0
—	—	28·0
JUPITER	52·0	52·0
SATURN	95·4	100·0
URANUS	191·8	196·0

The publication of this law could not fail to call attention to the existence of the space between Mars and Jupiter, which Kepler had already, a century and a half earlier, conjectured must be occupied by a planet, whose smallness alone rendered it invisible. The discovery of Uranus, in 1781, by Sir William Herschel, at a distance from the sun which agreed remarkably with Bode's law, appeared to add still greater probability to Kepler's conjecture. So keen did the interest become that an association of a number of astronomers was formed in Germany with the object of effecting the discovery of the supposed planet. The actual discovery, however, fell to the lot of Piazzi, the celebrated Italian astronomer. On the 1st January 1801 Piazzi, while carefully examining a part of the constellation Taurus, observed a star, which appeared on the following night to have changed its position with respect to the stars in its neighbourhood, showing, in fact, planetary motion. Subsequent observations confirmed the discovery, and the new planet was named Ceres by the discoverer. The elements of its orbit were later calculated by Gauss and showed that it really lay between those of Mars and Jupiter, and that its mean distance from the sun agreed with that assigned by Bode's law. Sir William Herschel measured its diameter and found it to be only 161 miles. It thus proved to be a very small object, though later determinations of its diameter make it somewhat larger than Sir William Herschel's result. The discovery of Ceres was followed in March 1802 by that of Pallas. This small planet was discovered by Olbers, who was then engaged in a series of observations of the newly discovered Ceres. The latter had by this time moved into the constellation Virgo, and here Olbers found an unknown star, which, after watching for some time, he found to have a motion amongst the stars. Like Ceres, Pallas also proved to be of small size, and to revolve round the sun in an orbit between Mars and Jupiter.

In consequence of the extreme smallness of the new planets, Ceres and Pallas, it was found that when any considerable length of time elapsed without an actual observation of them being made, some difficulty presented itself in picking them up again. Their discs are so small that they show little or no difference from the smaller stars seen in the field of the telescope. The necessity therefore became evident of mapping all the fixed stars in the region of the sky through which the planets moved. This laborious work was taken up by Harding at Lilienthal, and resulted, beside its primary object, in the discovery in 1804 of the third of the minor planets, to which Harding gave the name of Juno. A fourth was discovered by Olbers in 1807, and was named Vesta by Gauss, who calculated the elements of its orbit. There were thus in the early years of the nineteenth century four small planets already discovered revolving in the space between the orbits of Mars and Jupiter, where Kepler nearly two centuries earlier predicted a planet would be found.

Allusion has been made to the difficulty of recognising the small planets when any length of time has elapsed during which they have not been observed. Soon after the discovery of Ceres and Pallas, Olbers had suggested that they might possibly be the fragments of a larger planet, which, by the agency of some unknown convulsion, had been shattered at an earlier epoch. If this were so, the probability was great that many other small objects of the same kind would be discovered revolving in the same region of the solar system. This conjecture gave an immense impetus to planet seeking, and as an aid to the search stimulated exertion towards the production of complete maps or charts of the heaven containing not only the brighter stars, but also all stars down to the 10th magnitude. Important star maps had already been produced, amongst which we may mention those of Bayer, published in 1603, and those of the Rev. J. Flamstead in 1729. There were no charts, however, sufficiently comprehensive for the purpose now in view. Harding, one of the astronomers at the Observatory of Lilienthal, commenced the laborious work of supplying this want, and, in the course of his researches discovered Juno, as already referred to. His maps, under the title *Atlas Celestis*, appeared in 1822. Harding's *Atlas* was the first attempt made to represent the telescopic aspect of the heavens. His example was followed in 1825 by the Berlin Academy of Science, who produced charts of a zone of the celestial regions extending to 15° on each side of the equator.

Space will only permit of the mention of two other star maps from the list of those which have appeared since the publication of the Berlin zone. The most important maps with which the practical astronomer has yet been provided are undoubtedly those published by the Bonn Observatory between 1857-61. They include all stars down to magnitude 9·5 in the northern heavens, and a zone of 23´ south of the equator. These are still the reference maps used in all working observatories. Six maps published in 1855 by Mr Hind, and forming part of this volume, may be mentioned as suitable for the purposes of the amateur astronomer.

In recent years strenuous efforts are being made to produce star charts of the whole sky by photographic methods.

To return to the minor planets. The magnitude of the difficulty with which those astronomers had to contend who pinned their faith to the belief that many undiscovered members of this interesting family of planets existed may be estimated from the length of time which elapsed before any further success crowned their exertions. From the date of the discovery of Vesta in 1807 the search was kept up unremittingly, though with no appearance of encouragement till 1845, when the discovery of Astræa rewarded the unflagging perseverance of Hencke, an amateur astronomer residing at Driessen, in Germany. The next discovered was Hebe, in July 1847, a second reward of Hencke's indefatigable industry. To Great Britain belongs the credit of the next two discoveries, Iris and Flora having appeared to Mr Hind, who was then attached to Mr Bishop's observatory at Regent's Park, London, before the end of 1847. Metis was discovered by Mr Graham of the Markree Observatory in Ireland in April 1848, and Hygeia by M. de Gasparis of Naples in April of the following year. From this date the progress of discovery went on apace. Scarcely a single year has since passed without adding four or five, often more, new members to this interesting group of celestial bodies. Recently photography has been called in to the aid of the methods previously in use and has achieved noteworthy results.

It would probably not interest the reader to give a list of minor planets, the names of their discoverers, and the elements of their orbits, but a few particulars may be noted.

The periods of their revolution in their orbits about the sun vary from about three years to nearly nine years, and their mean distances, in round numbers, from 190,000,000 to 390,000,000 miles. Vesta, the brightest of them, is sometimes, when in opposition, as bright as a 6th magnitude star, and is thus visible to the naked eye. Ceres and Pallas are next in order of brightness. The diameters of the two largest are : 214 miles, that of Vesta ; and 196 miles, that of Ceres. The diameters of the smallest are difficult, if not impossible, to determine, but are said to be probably not more than from 5 to 15 miles. About 600 minor planets are now known, and the orbits of most of these have been computed. It is nearly certain that this number embraces all the larger members of the group. Further discoveries will therefore depend on the use of larger telescopes and more sensitive photographic plates.

CHAPTER VIII.

THE EARTH'S DISTANCE FROM THE SUN.

REFERENCE has already (p. 34) been made to the fact that the earth and the other planets revolve about the sun in elliptical orbits.

A series of observations of the sun's apparent diameter or a reference to an almanac would show that its value varies from about 32′ 35″ of arc to about 31′ 31″ of arc, with a mean value not very different from 32′. This variation of the angular diameter under which the sun is seen from the earth can only be accounted for on the supposition that the sun's distance constantly varies throughout the year. And it would be possible by actual measurement to determine the day of the year when the sun is nearest to us, and the day on which it is farthest from us. It is found that the diameter is greatest on the 1st January, when it measures 32′ 35″, and least on the 4th July, when 31′ 31″ is its amount. Its mean amount is 32′ 2·36″, as determined by thirty-three years' observations made at the Royal Observatory, Greenwich.

Hence the sun is nearest to us on the 1st January and at its greatest distance from us on the 4th July. It is at its mean distance on the 2nd April and 4th October, as shown by the fact that its diameter is on these days equal to the mean amount just stated. From these considerations the possibility of determining the relative distances of the sun at various dates is reached. Thus the greatest distance, the mean distance, and the least distance are proportional to the numbers 10,166, 10,000, and 9834. From which it appears that the greatest distance exceeds the mean by less than 2 per cent., while the least distance falls short of the mean by the same proportion. Again, in the midsummer of the northern hemisphere the earth is farthest from the sun, and nearest in midwinter. It would appear, therefore, that during the summer of the northern hemisphere the earth receives less heat from the sun than during the summer of the southern hemisphere. The difference is, however, quite insignificant, as will be seen when we consider the length of the seasons, as stated on p. 27. The summer half (northern) exceeds the winter half (southern summer) by over seven and a half days, a difference in time sufficient to compensate for the loss due to the greater distance. The varying distance of the sun has then nothing to do with the changes of temperature. These are due to the greater altitude of the sun above the horizon in summer as compared with that in winter, and to the fact that in summer the day —that portion of twenty-four hours during which heat is accumulating—is longer than the night, when heat is being lost.

So far nothing has been said as to the absolute distance of the sun from the earth. In what has been said above we have spoken only of the relative distances at different points of the earth's orbit. Reference, too, has been made on p. 31 to the proportionate distance of each planet of the solar system being dependent on its period of revolution about the sun. From this latter reference it follows that if the absolute distance of the earth from the sun were known, those of all the other planets from the sun would also be known. The sun's distance thus becomes of paramount importance as an astronomical problem, upon its accurate determination depending our knowledge of the absolute dimensions of the whole of the solar system. Determinations of the masses of the sun and planets depend on the distances between the body whose mass is under investigation and some other body whose movements are modified or perturbed by its attraction. The motion of every planet in its orbit is affected by the attraction of the neighbouring planets to an amount depending on the distances and masses. Hence it is impossible to predict with sufficient accuracy the position of a planet at any future time without a knowledge of these masses, nor to compute back its place for any epoch in the past. Not only this, the distances of a few of the fixed stars have been measured with a considerable degree of confidence, using the radius of the earth's orbit as the base line. Hence an accurate knowledge of the length of this line has long been looked upon as one of the most interesting objects of astronomical research. The history of the many attempts made to find the sun's distance is of much interest, showing, as it does, the progress of astronomical science step by step from the first attempts of the early ages to the vastly more accurate achievements of modern methods. The problem to find the distance of an inaccessible object is a comparatively simple one when we have a conveniently situated base line of sufficient length compared with the distance to be measured. We have only to measure by means of a sextant or a theodolite the angle at each end of the base line contained between that line and the lines from its ends to the inaccessible object. These two angles once determined, and the length of the base line known, we have the means either of laying down to scale on paper the triangle formed by the object, whose distance we want to determine, with the base, or of calculating the various parts of the triangle by mathematical formulæ. The lengths of the sides of the triangle give us the distance of the inaccessible object from each end of the base line. This is the method adopted for terrestrial objects. In fact, the knowledge of the two angles measured instrumentally enables us to determine the third angle, that at the object, which is simply equal to the difference of the directions in which the object is seen from the two ends of the base line, and is equivalent to the parallax of an astronomical object spoken of on p. 23.

When the distance of a celestial object is sought, the problem is complicated by the shortness of the only base line available, and the difficulties involved in the accurate measurements of very small angles. The moon being nearer to us than any other of the heavenly bodies presents the simplest form of the problem of finding the distance of a celestial object. For this purpose observations are made at two distant observatories nearly on the same meridian. The Zenith distance of the moon at the same moment is measured at both places, the latitudes of the observatories and the radius of the earth being known, we have then all the data necessary for determining the moon's distance from the centre of the earth. It need hardly be mentioned that even this simple form of the problem is greatly complicated in practice by the difficulty of finding two observatories on exactly the same meridian, and of making the observations at precisely the same moment. These difficulties can, however, be overcome by the introduction into the computations of the corrections necessary to reduce the observations to what they would have been if observed under ideal conditions.

In fig. 15, E is the centre of the earth, M the moon, O and P two observatories near the same meridian, one north, the other south, of the equator. From the observatory at O the moon will be seen projected on the sky amongst the stars at O^1, from P it will be seen at P^1. At each observatory its distance from a fixed star at the same moment, if possible, is measured, and the comparison of these measures provides the data for finding the angle at the moon's centre, subtended by the base line O P. Another method is to measure the zenith distances of the moon at each observatory at the same moment, that is, the angles M O Z and M P Z^1. The sum of these angles subtracted from the angle at E, which is known from the latitudes of the observatories, gives the angle at the moon. The observatory at the Cape of Good Hope was founded by the British Government originally for the solution of this problem.

Here the chord of the earth joining the two observatories is adopted as the base line, and as the moon's distance is only in round numbers about sixty times the radius of the earth, the problem is practicable, the parallax being comparatively

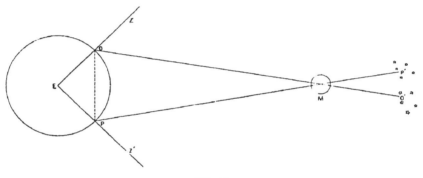

FIG. 15.

a large angle. To attempt, however, to measure the sun's distance by this method would be impossible, because the dimensions of the earth are so small compared with the distance, and the parallax, therefore, too small to be measured by any direct method. Quite different means must then be adopted. Ptolemy believed the sun's distance to be about nineteen times the distance of the moon, that is, about 1100 times the earth's radius, or about 4,500,000 miles. This value of the distance was adopted by all astronomers down to the time of Tycho Brahe and Copernicus, and would require the solar parallax, or the angle at the sun subtended by the earth's radius, to be about 3 minutes of arc. Kepler discussed this problem anew, making use of the observations of Tycho Brahe, and came to the conclusion that the sun's parallax did not exceed 1 minute of arc, and that its distance must be at least 13,500,000 miles, and that it was probably even greater. Modern observations and methods of attacking the problem have shown that these values were far from correct. They are valuable, however, as showing the impossibility of solving this difficult problem by any method of directly measuring the sun's parallax.

Cassini in 1672 made the first attempt, by the indirect method of investigating the parallax of the planet Mars. This planet in opposition is much nearer the earth than the sun is, hence its parallax is greater, and therefore a more easily measurable quantity. If once we know the parallax of Mars, and from it deduce its distance from the earth, we know also the distance of the sun from the earth and all the other planets, the proportion between these distances being known from Kepler's law, p. 34. Simultaneous observations were made by Cassini and others in France, and by Richer, who was sent by the French Academy of Science to Cayenne for this purpose. From a comparison of these observations, which consisted of a great number of measurements of the distance of the planet from the fixed stars close to it, the amount of displacement arising from the considerable distance between the places was ascertained, and from this the parallax of Mars in opposition was deduced.

Cassini's computations of the solar parallax from these observations gave a value of 9·5 seconds of arc, making the sun's distance from the earth 21,712 times the earth's radius, or 86,000,000 miles. The result is valuable and interesting, being, when compared with the old determinations, the first approximation to the true value which came at all near to a satisfactory solution of the problem. The sun's distance was still, however, very far from being definitely determined.

The intelligent reader may be excused for wondering that this noble problem has not been long since solved, and might feel inclined, when he sees the difference in the results which have been obtained with so much labour, to cast the blame on the astronomers, and point to these differences as exemplifying the imperfections of astronomical science, even in its modern state. But when we consider the difficulty of the problem, the wonder really is, not that astronomers have failed to measure the sun's distance with absolute certainty, but that they have been successful in obtaining even the vaguest ideas of what the distance amounts to. The earth's globe is so small compared with the distance of the sun that the angle to be measured, namely, that subtended by the earth's radius at the sun's centre, is equal to the angle a halfpenny, an inch in diameter, subtends at a distance of about 640 yards. The observations besides, at least in some cases, have to be made by different observers, under different climatic conditions, while all the time the earth is in motion in its orbit and is rotating on its axis. Again, the earth is not a perfect sphere, its equatorial radius been greater than its polar radius ; its orbit also is an ellipse, and therefore the sun's distance is not always the same.

Such are some of the difficulties with which the problem is surrounded. Some of them are of such a nature that corrections can be applied to reduce the results to what they would be for the equatorial radius and sun's mean distance. The parallax thus reduced is known as the sun's equatorial horizontal parallax.

It would be tedious to pass, even in brief review, all the methods by which attempts have been made to measure the sun's distance.

The orbit of the planet Venus lies in order of distance next nearer to the sun than the earth's. Hence, when Venus is nearest the earth, in inferior conjunction, a method similar to that used with Mars to obtain its parallax, and from it that of the sun, might have been adopted, if it had not been for the fact that Venus in inferior conjunction rises and sets nearly at the same time as the sun. Hence Venus is visible only under most unfavourable circumstances, in daylight, when the stars, except the very brightest, are invisible. It must be remembered that the position of the planet in such observations as these is fixed by measuring its distance from neighbouring stars.

However, Venus occasionally passes so directly between us and the sun that it moves across or transits the sun's disc appearing as a round black spot on the sun. Two methods have been devised for utilising these transits of Venus to determine the solar parallax.

As early as 1716 Halley suggested the following method. In fig. 16 suppose O and P be the positions of the observers, one as near the North Pole as possible, the other near the South. V, the planet, will be seen by observer O to transit the sun along the chord C Y D ; P will see it traverse the chord F X H. The distance X Y in miles between these two chords can be found, as the proportion between it and the distance O P between the observing stations is the same as the proportion between the distance of Venus from the sun and the distance of the earth from Venus—viz., about 66 to 25. If, then, we could find the angular distance X Y or the breadth of the zone between the two chords on the sun's disc, knowing the angular diameter of the sun by observation, we would have the proportion between X Y and the sun's absolute diameter, which we can thus determine in miles. Having now the sun's diameter in miles and its angular diameter, we have all the data necessary to determine its parallax and distance

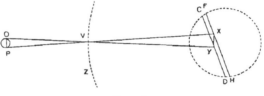

FIG. 16.

in miles. The solution of the problem then depends on the determination of the angular value of X Y, the breadth of the zone traced out on the sun's disc by Venus, as seen from the two stations. This can be computed from the lengths of the chords C Y D and F X H relatively to the sun's diameter, and to get these lengths we have to observe the times taken by Venus to traverse the chords, the rate of Venus' angular motion in its orbit being already well known. The problem thus finally resolves itself into the observation of the time taken by Venus to traverse the chords. In dealing with the details of the problem account must be taken of the earth's motion in its orbit, and of its rotation on its axis.

Delisle, in anticipation of the transit of Venus in 1761, devised a second method of finding the distance of the sun from the earth by means of it.

Suppose O and P, fig. 17, to be two stations at opposite sides of the earth nearly east and west of one another. Suppose V to be the position of Venus when it begins to transit the sun's disc as seen from O, and V^1 its position as seen later from P at the beginning of transit. Knowing the distance between O and P in miles, we can compute $V V^1$ in miles, because O P and $V V^1$ are proportional to the distances of the earth and of Venus from the sun. Now if the times of the beginning of transit be carefully observed, the difference between them is evidently the time Venus takes to travel along the arc $V V^1$. But the time it takes to travel round the whole orbit is also known. Hence we can find the length of the whole orbit in miles, and from this we can compute the radius of the orbit or the planet's mean distance. Knowing its mean distance we can compute the earth's mean distance from the proportion between the two as given by Kepler's law. In this method the observations necessary are the time of the beginning of transit as seen from a station where it begins earlier than at any other point of the earth's surface, or the earliest available, and the time of the beginning of transit as seen from a station where it begins as late as possible.

Similar observations may be made from stations where the transit ends earliest and latest. The absolute length of time between the beginnings or between the ends is what is required. The accuracy of the result depends, amongst other things, on an exact knowledge of the longitudes of the two stations and of the true local time, as well as accurate observations of the times of beginning or end of transit.

The transits which occurred in 1761 and 1769 were observed by numerous parties in different parts of the world. In the latter year the *Endeavour* was sent out under the command of Captain Cook by the British Government, and other expeditions were equipped by several European governments.

A new examination and comparison of the results of the two transits by

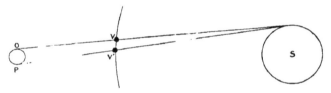

FIG. 17.

Professor Encke of Berlin (1822-24) brought out the value of the sun's equatorial horizontal parallax as 8·5776″, or the sun's distance 95,274,000 miles. This value was adopted by the various official *Nautical Almanacs*, amongst others the British, where it was retained up to 1869.

It may here be remarked, in view of the somewhat different value of the parallax accepted in still more recent years, that up to Encke's determination the tendency of all the successive researches had been one after the other to reduce the parallax, or, in other words, to increase the sun's distance ; all the old measures made the distance too small. Researches later than Encke's show that he brought out too great a distance.

In 1857 Airy urged the importance of further observations of Mars in opposition, especially at the oppositions of 1860, 1862, and 1877, which he considered most suitable, Mars being at these dates closer to the earth than usual. Leverrier also in 1861 showed that certain discrepancies in the theories of the movements of Venus, the earth, and Mars could not be reconciled with the 8·5776″ value of the solar parallax deduced by Encke, and thought it ought to be more nearly 8·95″. Observations were accordingly made in 1862 at Greenwich and at Williamstown, in Victoria, and were discussed by Mr Stone, then of the Greenwich Observatory. The result gave a parallax of 8·932″. In the same year independent observations were made at Pulkowa Observatory, in Russia, and at the Cape of Good Hope.

These were discussed by Winnecke, and gave 8·964″ as the result. A mean of these values is equivalent to a distance of about 91,430,000 miles.

These results were so satisfactory a corroboration of Leverrier's value, derived from his discussion of the theory of Venus, earth, and Mars, that his number 8·95″ was adopted in the British *Nautical Almanac* of 1870. The results so far obtained did not yet satisfy the requirements of modern astronomical science. Accordingly the transits of Venus of 1874 and 1882 were looked forward to with much interest, and vast preparations were made for their observation at all suitable points of the earth's surface, both by the usual telescopic methods and by new methods, in which photography played a considerable part. It would seem that as scientific requirements became more exacting, difficulties made their appearance, which in the earlier history of this inquiry were not considered of great importance, or were perhaps even unnoticed. Thus, in observations of Mars, the colour of the planet and the size of its disc were so different from the points of light presented to the observer by the stars with which the planet's position is compared, that the accuracy of the measures were liable to be affected with small errors. In the observations of Venus difficulties presented themselves from the distortion of the images of the planet and sun, the effect of refraction in the atmosphere of the planet. From this cause the exact moment of contact was not easily fixed upon by the observers ; in fact, instead of a simple, well-defined momentary contact, the edges of the planet and sun appeared to cling together for a considerable length of time.

When these difficulties were fully recognised they naturally created a feeling of want of confidence in the minds of astronomers as to the results of the methods hitherto adopted, and a number of new methods of attacking the problem of the sun's distance were soon suggested. Of these we need only refer to that by observation of the parallax of some one or other of the minor planets. These small objects, unlike Mars, present in the telescope an appearance exactly similar to that of the stars by which they are surrounded, and from which their distances have to be measured. They never come so close to the earth as either Mars or Venus, and therefore their parallax is smaller, but this disadvantage is said to be amply compensated for by their stellar appearance in the telescope. One of the recently discovered planets, Eros, appears to remove the objection due to distance, as it sometimes comes nearer to the earth than the orbit of Mars.

The following table, taken from Professor Simon Newcomb's work on the *Fundamental Constants of Astronomy*, published at Washington in 1895, gives the results of his discussion of some of the best values of the solar parallax, and the methods by which they were obtained :—

From observations of Mars by Gill at Ascension Island .	8·780″
From Pulkowa determination of the constant of aberration	8·793″
From contacts in transits of Venus	8·794″
From other determinations of the constant of aberration .	8·806″
From heliometer observations of the minor planets .	8·807″
From measurements of the distance of Venus from the sun's centre	8·857″

From these and other determinations Professor Newcomb brings out a mean value for the solar parallax of 8·80″. This value has recently been adopted by the *Nautical Almanac,* and corresponds to a distance of 92,897,000 miles. It would at first sight appear that there was nothing further to be desired in the accuracy with which the sun's distance is now known. It must be remembered, however, that a difference of one-hundredth of a second of arc in the sun's parallax is equivalent to more than 100,000 miles in the sun's distance from the earth. It is much to be desired, therefore, that the parallax should be known with certainty to within half-a-hundredth of a second of arc. The discovery of the minor planet Eros by Herr G. Witt of Berlin in 1898 is expected to clear off some of the remaining uncertainty. Eros was discovered on a photograph of a part of the sky in the neighbourhood of the star β Aquarii, and turned out to be of considerably greater interest than it would have received as an ordinary member of the family of minor planets.

We have referred at some length (p. 37) to the discovery of these bodies. Eros, one of the smallest of the group, its diameter being estimated at only 17 miles, is in no way peculiar except that when it is in perihelion—that is, nearest the sun—it comes inside the orbit of Mars, though its orbit lies partly outside or farther from the sun than that of Mars. If at the same time it is in opposition to the sun as seen from the earth, it approaches nearer to us than any other member of the planetary system, including Venus. When the latter planet is most favourably situated—that is, farthest from the sun, between the earth and sun, with the earth in its nearest position to the sun—it may approach us within 25,000,000 miles. Mars, on the other hand, when nearest the sun, in opposition, and with the earth farthest from the sun, can only approach within about 35,000,000 miles of us. Eros, however, may approach us much closer than either, for if its opposition takes place when it is in perihelion and the earth in aphelion, it may approach to within 13,000,000 miles of us. The parallax is therefore larger and more easily measured than that of either Venus or Mars. At the International Astrographic Congress held in Paris in 1900, resolutions were passed aiming at systematising the work to be done, by the various observatories co-operating with the Conference, during the following autumn and winter at the favourable opposition of Eros then to take place. As a result of this co-operation a large number of photographic and other observations has been secured, and the mass of calculations required is still under discussion. Though the final result has not yet been announced, there is good reason to expect that the parallax and distance of the sun will be determined with a degree of accuracy hitherto unattainable. Some provisional results from a small number of plates appear to show that the solar parallax derived from the observations of Eros will not differ much from the present accepted value, 8·80″.

Eros revolves round the sun in 642 days; its mean distance from the sun is 135,309,000 miles, or more than 6,000,000 miles less than the mean distance of Mars. The eccentricity of its orbit is 0·2114, somewhat greater than that of the orbit of Mercury. From this value of the eccentricity it appears that the distance of Eros from the sun may vary from about 107,000,000 miles to 164,000,000 miles. The inclination of its orbit to the ecliptic is 9° ·57′.

CHAPTER IX.

PHYSICAL CONSTITUTION OF THE SUN.

WHEN the sun is seen through haze thick enough to protect the eyes from the excessive effulgence of its rays, or when viewed through coloured glass of sufficient density to absorb a great part of its light, it presents the appearance of a uniformly coloured circular disc. When a telescope of moderate power is used, which it is important to remember must have its eye-piece provided with densely coloured glass to prevent injury to the eye, it will generally be found that there are dark spots on the surface of irregular form and of different sizes, sometimes arranged in groups, sometimes separated by intervals at different parts of the disc. If sufficient magnifying power be used, the more conspicuous spots will be found to consist of a central nucleus darker than the rest of the spot, surrounded by a less dark region known as the penumbra. In the parts of the sun's disc in the neighbourhood of spots, especially when the spots are arranged in extensive groups, smaller bright patches of light are seen, more luminous than the general surface. These are called faculæ, or torches. Faculæ are sometimes also seen in the region where spots have disappeared. Besides the faculæ, a somewhat more recent discovery has shown the whole of the sun's surface to be diversified by small patches of light, of definite form and systematic arrangement, to which the appellation of willow leaves has been given.

When the spots are examined carefully it is found that their structure is subject to extensive, often excessively rapid changes. Sometimes two neighbouring spots will coalesce to form one, at other times a single spot of large dimensions will break up into two or more. Observations extending over several days will show that the spots appear to move across the sun's disc from east to west. Sometimes they make their first appearance at the eastern edge of the disc, move across it and disappear on the western edge, crossing the disc in a period of about twelve days, reappearing after a somewhat longer period on the eastern edge. Occasionally, however, spots appear inside the disc, follow their course towards the west for a few days, and then disappear. Astronomers have concluded that these spots are situated on the sun's surface, and that their apparent motion across the sun is only to be explained by the rotation of the sun on an axis. Further, it has been seen that the apparent paths of the spots are at certain parts of the year straight lines, and at other times curved lines. Thus in February the paths are curved upwards, as in fig. 18 ; in June they are in straight lines with a downward inclination towards the west. In September they are curved downwards, and in December they are again straight lines, but with an upward inclination towards the west. Careful consideration of these observations has led to the conclusion that the sun rotates on its axis in a mean period of twenty-five days nine hours. The accuracy of this result is, however, uncertain, because the spots have been found to have a slight motion of their own on the sun's surface, in addition to their apparent motion with the sun's rotation. It has also more recently been found that spots situated nearest the sun's equator cross the disc in somewhat shorter time than those in higher solar latitudes. From the curved form of the path it has been shown that the sun's equator is inclined to the ecliptic at an angle of $7°\ 15'$. This latter conclusion will appear more simple if we imagine for a moment what would take place if there were no such inclination of the sun's equator to the ecliptic. The result would be that the path of a spot which crossed the sun's disc would at all times of the year be a perfectly straight line. The curvature in February and September shows, therefore, that the sun's equator is inclined towards the north side of the ecliptic, or upwards, in February, and downwards, or towards the south side, in September. These curves afford, when at their maximum, a means of measuring the amount of the inclination. In June and December the earth in its revolution in its orbit about the sun crosses the plane of the sun's equator, and the spots then appear to traverse the disc in

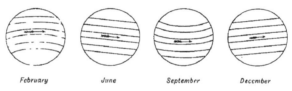

February   June   September   December

FIG. 18.

straight lines. The claim to priority of discovery of the spots is a somewhat disputed point. There appears to be no doubt, however, that they were independently discovered by Galileo and by John Fabricius early in the year 1611, and by Christopher Scheiner, a professor in the University of Ingolstadt, a few months later. Both of the earlier discoverers, reasoning from the motion of the spots across the sun's disc, came to the conclusion that the sun rotates on its axis. Galileo went somewhat further, and made the first determinations of the period of the rotation, and the angle by which the sun's equator is inclined to the ecliptic.

To Scheiner is due the first intimation of the division of the better defined spots into nucleus and penumbra. The character of the spots and the mysterious changes which are constantly going forward on the surface of our luminary have, it need not be said, attracted the attention of modern astronomers to a degree which cannot be considered other than natural, when we remember the enormous influence the sun exercises on the operations of nature on our globe. It is impossible to suppose that the human mind, ever eager to solve the problems of nature, and to sound the depths of the unknown, would rest content till every effort had been made to discover the character and origin of the solar spots, and the influence they exert on our surroundings. Hence no question of astronomical physics has been more discussed than the problem presented

D

by these phenomena. At an early date it was seen that the spots are usually to be found within a zone of the sun's surface extending about 35° on each side of the equator. Outside this zone, towards the polar regions, spots are rarely seen. They appear also to be less numerous in the immediate vicinity of the equator. This circumstance seemed to Sir John Herschel to imply that the spots owed their origin to gyratory movements in the sun's atmosphere, depending on the rotation of that body on its axis. He considered them analogous in some particulars, though not in all, to the trade winds, caused in the earth's equatorial regions by the transference of heated air from the equator to the poles, modified by the earth's rotation on its axis. The difference of temperature of the air at the equator and the poles is due to a cause external to the earth, namely, the greater heating effect of the sun's rays at the equator. There is no external cause to account for such a transference of the sun's atmosphere, but Sir John Herschel accounted for it in the following manner: Owing to the sun's rotation, its atmosphere rotating with it assumes a protuberant form at the equator. There is, thus, a greater thickness of atmosphere at the equator than at the poles, the effect of which is that the hotter layers of the sun situated below the atmosphere receive an amount of

Fig. 19.

protection from cooling by radiation. Hence he supposed the difference of temperature to arise which would possibly be sufficient to account for the transference of the solar atmosphere from the equator to the poles. Combined with the rotation, effects similar to hurricanes and tornadoes would be produced, the upper currents tearing apart the overlying layers of the atmosphere, and thus partially exposing the opaque surface of the sun below. In later years the revelations made by the spectroscope have thrown new light on many of Herschel's conjectures as to the solar constitution.

Alexander Wilson, Professor of Astronomy in the University of Glasgow, had already shown that the spots were cavities in the sun's surface. This idea was revealed to him by the examination of an unusually large spot which appeared on the sun's surface in 1769. He watched it day after day moving from the centre to the western edge; there he found the penumbra first thinning on the side of the spot lying towards the centre of the disc, then it disappeared altogether. This is precisely what would happen if the spot were really a cavity and it were gradually turned by the sun's rotation, till the spectator could no longer look straight into it, but viewed it by looking over the nearer edge. As the penumbra contracted the whole spot narrowed in the direction of the sun's radius, as one should expect it to do when seen in perspective. Wilson awaited its reappearance on the sun's eastern edge, and when it again became visible he found the same effects of perspective, the penumbra being now narrowed on the opposite side. The original form of the spot when first seen returned as it approached the sun's centre. Fig. 19 illustrates the change in the appearance of a spot due to the sun's rotation. Exception has, however, been taken to this explanation of the sun-spots by later observers, but the difficulty of finally deciding the question is great, owing to the generally disturbed state of the spots, and the rapid changes which often take place in their structure, during their passage from the sun's centre to the edge.

In 1843 Schwabe of Dessau announced his discovery that the number of spots appearing on the sun's surface was subject to a periodic fluctuation, gradually falling from a maximum to a minimum, and increasing again to a maximum in about ten years. Later observations have shown that the period is a little more than eleven years. The importance of this discovery did not immediately gain the attention it deserved. Schwabe, however, continued his observations, and was finally awarded the gold medal of the Royal Astronomical Society in 1857.

To Dr Rudolph Wolf of Berne and Zurich is due the credit of determining the eleven year period, from an exhaustive investigation of the whole series of sun-spot observations, beginning with those of Galileo, and of proving that it corresponds exactly with the period which has been shown to exist in the frequency of magnetic disturbances in the earth's surface.

Many other manifestations of the working of nature on the earth and in its atmosphere have with more or less certainty been supposed to show a periodicity similar to that of the sun-spots. The manifestations of aurora or northern lights have without doubt such a periodicity. But the attempts which have been made to trace a connection between the sun-spots and the phenomena of weather, or the price of corn so far as this depends on the recurrence of good and bad seasons, have not been so successful as the probability of such a connection might have led one to expect. This is no doubt due to the inherent difficulties of such researches, various incidental circumstances interfering with the recurrence of such phenomena in regular sequence.

Schwabe's discovery of the periodicity of sun-spots created an outburst of enthusiasm in the direction of researches into the physical nature of the sun. The progress made by spectroscopic analysis in the third quarter of the nineteenth century still further increased the interest in the study of solar phenomena. The various eclipse expeditions of the latter half of the century, and the establishment of observatories specially equipped for physical research are the natural outcome of this enthusiasm.

At the present date the general consensus of astronomical opinion regards the sun as composed of a central mass of intensely heated matter, surrounded by a shell of luminous clouds, to which the name of photosphere has been given, and which constitutes the visible surface of the sun. Outside the photosphere lies a red stratum of gaseous matter known as the chromosphere; outside this again is the corona, consisting of a halo of pearly rays seen only during the brief moments of a total solar eclipse, stretching out from the sun's edge to a distance equal to several times the sun's diameter.

Of the constitution of the vast interior mass little is known for certain. It must be supposed, however, that being the source of the energy constantly radiating from the sun's surface in the form of light and heat, it is necessarily itself in a state of intense heat. From the solar parallax of 8·80″ it can be computed that the sun's diameter is about 866,000 miles, or about 109 times the diameter of the earth. In extent the sun, therefore, exceeds the earth no less than 1,304,000 times. Its absolute mass or quantity of matter contained within these enormous proportions has been shown to be about 328,000 times that of the earth. Hence the sun's mean density is only equal to one quarter of that of the earth.

As the result of spectroscopic research more is known of the constituents of the photosphere. This shell of luminous matter surrounding the sun is formed by the cooling due to the radiation of heat into the cold regions of outer space, and the consequent condensation of the gases near the outer surface of the sun. The chromospheric shell is composed mainly of hydrogen gas, and from its surface rise up the great eruptions of cloudy flames known as the red prominences or protuberances.

Very little is as yet known of the corona, except that it is certainly of solar origin, a fact which was revealed by photography during eclipses about 1860. ·Previous to this the corona was generally supposed to be due either to refraction at the edge of the moon, or to the earth's atmosphere.

As a great deal of our knowledge of the sun's physical condition is the result of the spectroscopic study of its light, it is as well here to make a brief survey of the facts of spectrum analysis.

Newton discovered that white light was composed of rays of various colours. If a beam of sunlight be allowed to pass through a prism it is refracted or turned out of the straight line in which it had before travelled. A prism may be described as a block of glass, or other material, with three parallel edges and two triangular ends. The sunlight in passing through the glass is bent towards the base of the prism. The component rays are, however, not all equally bent or refracted ; the red is less refracted than the yellow, the yellow than the green, and the violet is more refracted than any of the other colours. Of course the increase of the refraction is gradual from the beginning of the red to the end of the violet, the colours blending into one another gradually. There is no abrupt difference of refrangibility between any one colour and another. Hence, besides the refraction which results from the passage of sunlight through a prism, we have also dispersion of the light into its component rays. Now if a screen be brought into the path of the light after it has passed through the prism, instead of the simple image of the original aperture through which the light was admitted, we have a continuous band of light of all colours from red to violet, known as the spectrum. It was not till the beginning of the nineteenth century that Wollaston and Fraunhofer independently showed that if the aperture through which the sunlight is admitted to the prism is a narrow slit placed parallel to the edge of the prism, the resulting spectrum of sunlight is crossed by a number of dark lines. The discovery of these dark lines, which are still known as Fraunhofer's lines, may be considered the birth of the science of spectrum analysis. It was not, however, till the second half of the century that the meaning of the Fraunhofer lines was explained and the new science placed on a solid foundation. The spectroscope can be arranged in many ways to suit the particular purpose for which it is intended. In all its forms, however, the essential part is the prism, or combination of several prisms. All the other parts of the instrument are introduced for the purpose of throwing the light on the prism in the most advantageous way, or for examining the light most conveniently after it has been passed through the instrument. Sometimes instead of a prism or prisms a diffraction grating is used. This is a piece of glass or metal on which a large number, amounting to many thousands, of parallel lines have been ruled. When light is reflected from such a grating it is dispersed and forms a spectrum, essentially the same, though differing in certain details, from the prismatic spectrum. As arranged for astronomical purposes, the spectroscope is fitted with a collimator and viewing telescope, and is attached to the eye end of an equatorially mounted telescope. The collimator is simply a lens in the focus of which the slit is placed. If, now, an image of any luminous object be formed on the slit, the light emerges from the lens in a beam of parallel rays. This beam then passes through the prism, or is reflected from the surface of the diffraction grating, and the spectrum so formed is examined in the viewing telescope. To bring the image of the luminous object on the slit the spectroscope is attached to the eye-piece of the telescope, and the slit is adjusted carefully in the focus of the object glass if a refractor is used, or of the mirror if we use a reflecting telescope. In this way the light of the sun, planets, and stars can be examined. If, instead of sunlight, we wish to examine the light of a candle or lamp, or of the incandescent lime cylinder, we of course dispense with the telescope, and simply throw the light directly on the slit of the spectroscope. We will then find that the spectrum of either of these lights consists of a continuous band of colour ranging from red to violet. The spectrum of sunlight differs from this in having a large number of dark lines drawn across it of various thicknesses. These are the Fraunhofer lines, many of which were mapped by him. He also affixed designations to the most conspicuous of them, using the letters of the alphabet for this purpose. These are still known as the A line, the B line, the D line, and so on. Again, if we examine the light of a Bunsen's burner in which some salt of one or other of the metals has been volatilized, we will find that the spectrum consists of bright lines, in every case characteristic of the particular substance which has been introduced into the burner. Thus, if we use a salt of sodium, such as common salt (chloride of sodium), we find a spectrum of one bright line in the yellow, or of two lines close together if the spectroscope is sufficiently powerful. If a salt of lithium be used, a spectrum consisting principally of two bright lines, one red and one orange, is shown. Strontium gives a spectrum of several bright lines—red, orange, and blue. Cæsium of two blue lines. Thus it will be seen that there are three varieties of spectra—(1) the continuous spectrum shown by the candle flame and limelight. This spectrum is exhibited by all solid and liquid bodies in a state of incandescence, also by gases in a condition of great pressure. It must be remembered that the light from a candle is due to the incandescence of solid particles of carbon in the flame. (2) The bright line spectrum, such as that shown by salts of the metals volatilized in the Bunsen burner. Gases at ordinary pressure, and vapours when incandescent, show discontinuous spectra consisting of bright lines. (3) The spectrum crossed by dark lines, of which the solar spectrum is typical.

Sir David Brewster in 1822 made a remarkable experiment, which showed that dark lines could be produced in a continuous spectrum by absorption. He interposed a vessel containing nitrous gas between a prism and a source of light which of itself would give a continuous spectrum. He at once saw that the spectrum was now crossed by dark lines, somewhat similar to Fraunhofer lines. To the great German physicist Kirchhoff is due the honour of establishing fully the relationship between the dark lines due to absorption and the bright lines of the gaseous spectra. He found that when sunlight was passed through a flame containing sodium, the two close dark lines of the solar spectrum, to which Fraunhofer affixed the letter D, were exhibited with increased intensity of blackness, though when the sunlight was screened off and the light of the sodium flame alone allowed to reach the spectroscope the two yellow lines appeared as usual. He also found that if the light of the incandescent lime lamp be passed through the sodium flame its continuous spectrum will be crossed by the two dark D lines, and if the light be passed through a flame in which lithium is volatilized, the lithium lines appear as dark lines in the spectrum. Similar results followed the examination of various other substances. Kirchhoff was thus led to formulate the general law that when light from a solid or liquid incandescent body is passed through an incandescent gas of lower temperature, those parts of the continuous spectrum are absorbed which are of the same refrangibility as the bright lines of the spectrum of the gas, so that we get a spectrum of dark lines on a bright background, the dark lines being in precisely the same positions in the spectrum as the bright lines occupied in the spectrum of the gas.

These experiments provide us at once with the explanation of the existence of dark lines in the solar spectrum. If we suppose the sun to consist of a central incandescent body, whether of solid, liquid, or of gaseous matter at high pressure, surrounded by an atmosphere containing the incandescent vapours of various metallic and other substances at a lower temperature, then these vapours, by absorbing those parts of the light of the incandescent body which they themselves would emit, will produce the well-known dark lines in the solar spectrum. If, now, it could be shown on careful examination that the bright lines of the spectrum of any substance corresponded exactly to dark lines in the solar spectrum, we would be justified in supposing that substance to form one constituent of the solar atmosphere. We have already referred to the experimental proof of this in the case of sodium. Kirchhoff by similar methods, but worked out in minute detail, to which it is impossible to refer here, has proved the existence in the solar atmosphere of iron, calcium, magnesium, and many other substances in a state of vapour or gas. In order to prove with certainty the connection between the bright line spectra of various bodies and the dark Fraunhofer lines of the solar spectrum, the following device has been adopted. Sunlight is admitted through one half only of the slit of the spectroscope, the other half being covered by a small reflecting prism or mirror, so arranged that the light from the incandescent vapour or gas under examination can be reflected into this half of the slit, and thus through the collimator to the prism. There are thus two beams of light entering the spectroscope side by side, and forming their spectra in juxtaposition, and under precisely similar conditions of refraction and dispersion. If, now, it is found that the bright lines of the gaseous spectrum agree exactly with the corresponding dark lines of the solar spectrum, we must conclude that these particular dark lines are caused by absorption in the solar atmosphere, due to the presence there in a state of vapour of the substance under examination.

The following list, which is taken from Professor C. A. Young's *Sun*, contains the names of the elements which have been identified in the solar spectrum by

Kirchhoff, Angstrom, Thalen, Lockyer, and others, and the number of lines which have been shown to belong to each :—

Iron	.	. 460	Hydrogen	.	.	5
Titanium	.	. 118	Palladium	.	.	5
Calcium .	.	. 75	Vanadium	.	.	4
Manganese	.	. 57	Molybdenum	.	.	4
Nickel .	.	. 33	Strontium	.	.	4
Cobalt .	.	. 19	Lead .	.	.	3
Chromium	.	. 18	Uranium	.	.	3
Barium .	.	. 11	Aluminium	.	.	2
Sodium .	.	. 9	Cerium .	.	.	2
Magnesium	.	. 7	Cadmium	.	.	2
Copper (?)	.	. 7 ?)	Oxygen .	.	.	—

The last of these elements, oxygen, depends for its identification on the coincidence of some of the bright lines of its spectrum with bright bands, not dark lines, in the solar spectrum. This discovery is due to Dr Henry Draper and Dr Schuster, but the interpretation of the coincidences has met with the dissent of some other eminent authorities.

Besides the elements contained in the above list, there are several others which are with greater or less probability believed to be present in the sun. A few have failed to show the slightest trace of their presence after the most careful examination both of the ordinary spectrum and that of the chromosphere. The apparent absence of these has led to much discussion, and would appear to be most simply explained by the supposition that though they are elementary substances as known on the earth, they are not really so, but are composed of two or more elements. They are classed as terrestrial elements, because we have no means of dissociating the simpler elements of which they are composed. The greater heat to which they are subjected in the sun may, however, be capable of effecting this dissociation.

The late Professor Rowland of the Johns Hopkins University, Baltimore, by a photographic investigation of the solar spectrum has proved the existence of thirty-six terrestrial elements in the sun. His results were arrived at by photographic comparisons of the spectra of all the known elements, except a few very rare ones and a few of the gaseous elements, with the spectrum of the sun.

The following list of the thirty-six elements shown to exist in the sun was published by Professor Rowland in 1891, as a preliminary list only, and is arranged according to intensities :—

Calcium.	Strontium.	Copper.
Iron.	Vanadium.	Zinc.
Hydrogen.	Barium.	Cadmium.
Sodium.	Carbon.	Cerium.
Nickel.	Scandium.	Glucinum.
Magnesium.	Yttrium.	Germanium.
Cobalt.	Zirconium.	Rhodium.
Silicon.	Molybdenum.	Silver.
Aluminium.	Lanthanum.	Tin.
Titanium.	Niobium.	Lead.
Chromium.	Palladium.	Erbium.
Manganese.	Neodymium.	Potassium.

The number of lines identified by Professor Rowland with lines in the spectrum of iron amounts to 2000 or more. The calcium lines number at least 75, while the copper lines are reduced to 2. To carbon he assigned 200 or more. The magnesium lines number 20, those of sodium 11, and of aluminium 4. There are eight elements, the evidence for whose existence in the sun Professor Rowland considered doubtful—viz., iridium, platinum, thorium, uranium, osmium, ruthenium, tantalum, tungsten ; and fifteen others for the existence of which he found no evidence in the solar spectrum—viz., gold, mercury, phosphorus, sulphur, nitrogen, boron, bismuth, arsenic, antimony, cæsium, indium, rubidium, selenium, thallium, and praseodymium. It must not be supposed, however, that these latter elements are proved to be absent from the sun. On the contrary, Professor Rowland remarks, that, "were the whole earth heated to the temperature of the sun, its spectrum would probably resemble that of the sun very closely." This investigation of the solar spectrum was carried out with so much care, and with such powerful instruments, that the results, though preliminary only, must be considered of great authority.

Analysis of the light of the chromosphere shows that this solar envelope is composed chiefly of glowing hydrogen, though sodium, magnesium, and some other metals are also present occasionally. The red prominences or protuberances are connected with the chromosphere. They are shown to belong to the solar atmosphere by the fact that the moon passes over them gradually in the solar eclipse.

Unlike the spots which are found most frequently in two zones of the sun's surface, reaching from 10° to 35° of solar latitude N. and S., the protuberances are to be seen at all points of the sun's edge, and doubtless exist all over the surface. They are, however, to be found most abundantly in those latitudes in which spots are also most frequent. It is therefore generally supposed that there may be some sort of connection between sun-spots and protuberances. The connection is much more intimate between protuberances and faculæ, those curious bright streaks seen to best advantage near the edge of the sun's disc.

Protuberances are often of vast extent, reaching from 5000 to 30,000 miles outside the sun's edge, and occasionally as much as 80,000. On one or two occasions a height of even 300,000 miles or more has been recorded.

The chromosphere lies outside the photosphere, which constitutes the visible surface of the sun, and the chief source of its light and heat. It appears to overlie the photosphere in the form of gigantic streams of flaming hydrogen spreading out over the surface, and frequently bursting upwards in enormous masses, forming the red prominences rising above the general level of the surface, portions often separating from the chromosphere and floating upwards into the coronal regions. The existence of the chromosphere and prominences was known early in the eighteenth century, having been seen by several observers during the progress of total eclipses. Universal attention was directed to them after the eclipse of 1842, when the extreme brilliance of the prominences was a marked feature. Much discussion followed as to their solar or lunar origin. The eclipse of 1851, seen in Norway and Sweden, left little doubt that they were solar appendages, and to some extent proved that the substance of which they were composed formed a continuous stratum over the sun's surface. The eclipse of 1860 finally settled the question of their solar origin, the photographs of Mr Warren de la Rue (shown in Plate V., figs. 4, 5, and 6) revealing them gradually covered and uncovered by the moon during the eclipse. The invention of the spectroscope previous to the eclipse of 1868 enabled their chemical nature to be determined. It was then found that their spectrum consisted of bright lines, of which the chief were those of hydrogen. It soon after occurred to Jannsen and Lockyer, independently, that by means of a suitably arranged spectroscope, the prominences could be seen without an eclipse in full sunlight. The possibility of doing so depends on the different effect which the use of several prisms, instead of a single prism, has on the bright line spectrum. If the light of the continuous spectrum be passed through a number of prisms, one after the other, the result is that the whole spectrum is lengthened, and the light consequently weakened, by being spread over so much more surface. With the bright line spectrum, however, this is not the case; the spectrum is indeed lengthened as the result of the lines being separated farther from one another, but the light having been once analysed into bright lines, each consisting of mono-chromatic or simple light, undergoes no further change from increased dispersive power of the spectroscope. It follows that the general illumination from sunlight, which enters the spectroscope along with the light of the prominences, will be so weakened, if the dispersive power is sufficient, that the portion of a prominence whose image falls on the slit can be seen by means of any one of the bright lines of the spectrum, and the form of the prominence may be traced by bringing different parts of it on the slit in succession, or by widening the slit sufficiently to admit the image of the whole or a considerable part of the prominence.

In Plate III. a few illustrations are given of the form of the prominences, taken from the *Memoirs of the Italian Spectroscopic Society*, by kind permission of the editor. The five sketches on the right show various stages in the formation and disappearance of a prominence seen by the Rev. J. Fenyi at the Observatory of Kalocsa, in Hungary, from 10 hours 15 minutes to 12 hours 38 minutes, on 24th December 1894. The second and third of these five sketches were made at 11 hours 20 minutes and 11 hours 55 minutes respectively, the prominence during this interval having increased outward from the sun's edge to three times its former dimensions. At its maximum its length was equal to nearly seven-tenths of the sun's radius, or about 290,000 miles. In the two following sketches the prominence is seen rapidly disappearing. The illustration on the left shows a prominence seen by Professor Tacchini at Rome in November 1892, which attained to a height of some 160,000 miles. The remaining prominence was seen by Professor Tacchini in February 1895.

The corona can be seen only when the sun is totally eclipsed. Unlike the prominences, which by the spectroscopic method can now be seen in full daylight, no method has yet been devised for exhibiting the corona, unless during the short interval, never exceeding five or six minutes, when the brilliance of the sun's light is eclipsed by the intervention of the moon's body. Attempts have been made in this direction, but hitherto without any very satisfactory result. Before the introduction of photography into the regular work of astronomical observations, the form of the corona was known only by drawings depicted by various observers, with or without telescopic assistance. The character of the phenomenon, however, is such as to make the execution of drawings a matter of extreme difficulty and uncertainty. Two observers side by side have frequently produced pictures which could hardly be supposed to represent the same phenomenon. Differences in the sensitiveness of their eyes, and possibly the attention of each being attracted by what seemed to him the most striking feature, the shortness of the time of totality requiring that much of the detail should be filled in from memory, all tend to such a result. The photographic method has been employed with greater success, though even with its aid it is impossible to depict all the minute details of the complicated structure, especially in the outermost extensions, where the light is weaker. On the whole, however, photographs are more to be trusted than drawings. In Plate V. the form of the corona is illustrated by three examples. That of 1871 is taken from the *Memoirs of the Royal Astronomical Society*, Vol. XLI., by permission of the Society, and is from a series of photographs made in India by Mr Davis for the Earl of Crawford. A drawing of the combined photographs was made, and from this the illustration has been reproduced. The illustration of the corona of 1896 is reproduced from the *Memoirs of the Italian Spectroscopic Society*, by permission of the editor. The original is from a drawing made from photographs taken at Nova Zembla by the members of the Pulkowa Observatory expedition. That of the 28th May 1900 is from an original photograph taken by a member of the Scottish expedition to Santa Pola in Spain.

It will at once strike the reader that a considerable change takes place in the corona from year to year, giving it quite a different character at the various eclipses. In all of the illustrations it will be seen that the coronal light in the neighbourhood of the sun's poles is shorter, and contains more detail of a feathery character than that round the remainder of the sun's disc. About the equatorial regions the streams of light are usually much longer, extending outwards to sometimes as much as three solar diameters from the sun's edge. Photographs taken at successive eclipses during the last thirty years or so show clearly that there is an intimate connection between the form of the corona and the prevalence of sun-spots. At the sun-spot maximum the corona is on a grander scale, the long extensions occupy nearly the whole circumference of the disc, while the shorter plume-like tufts are confined to a small portion only of the edge immediately about the sun's poles. The 1871 eclipse is a good example of this form. At the sun-spot minimum, on the other hand, the long streams of light are only seen about the equatorial regions, and the shorter plumes reach on each side of the poles to a greater angular distance along the edge. The eclipse of 1900 is a good example of a corona of the sun-spot minimum form.

The question as to whether the corona was of solar, lunar, or terrestrial atmospheric origin was for long in doubt, but was settled by the independent observations of Professor Harkness and Professor C. A. Young of New Jersey, who found that the spectrum of the corona of 1869 contained a bright green line. This observation could only be interpreted to mean that the corona was composed partly at least of incandescent gas, and therefore must be of solar origin. Photographs taken at far distant stations support this conclusion by their precise agreement in the details of the coronal structure. Besides the green line just referred to, the spectrum of the corona contains the bright lines of hydrogen. The origin of the green line is up to the present unknown. There are also seen some traces of a continuous spectrum, crossed by a few of the dark lines of the solar spectrum. This fact proves that, besides the incandescent gases of which the corona is principally composed, it also contains minute particles of matter in a form capable of reflecting the solar light.

As to the origin of the substance of which the corona is composed, the reason of the various forms it assumes on different occasions, and its connection with the periodicity of sun-spots, much remains to be discovered. As, however, opportunities for the study of the corona occur only at rare intervals, and are then only of two or three minutes' average duration, progress in this line of discovery must necessarily be slow.

In Plate III. the solar disc is represented as seen under low magnifying power, showing groups of spots. A portion of the disc is represented in the same Plate under high magnifying power showing several spots, large and small, accompanied by faculæ. The more conspicuous appearance of the faculæ near the sun's edge is well shown in this figure, resulting from the diminution of the sun's light over that part of the disc. In Plate III. we have also a representation of the apparent magnitude of the sun as seen from the various planets. To an observer on Mercury the sun would be seen with an apparent diameter of about a degree and a half, or about three times the diameter under which it is seen by the inhabitants of the earth. To an inhabitant of Mercury the sun's disc would, therefore, appear nine times as great as it appears to us. Seen from Venus the apparent size is much smaller than from Mercury, but still larger than as seen from the earth. To all the other planets it presents a smaller apparent disc, decreasing till Neptune, the planet farthest from the sun, is reached, to whose inhabitants it would appear with a diameter of only one minute of arc, about the diameter of Venus as seen from the earth when she is in inferior conjunction.

CHAPTER X.

THE moon is the earth's only satellite or attendant in our annual journey round the sun. It is the nearest to us of all the heavenly bodies, and with the sole exception of the sun interests us more than any of them, exciting the greatest popular curiosity, as well as presenting to the serious student of Astronomy most fascinating problems. The succession of its phases must have engaged the attention of mankind from the earliest ages, and has suggested a division of time intermediate between the day and the year, which, though somewhat inconvenient on account of its variability, has still so much practical value as to secure its continued endurance. The rapidity of the moon's motion among the stars renders observation of it most useful to travellers and seamen, for the purpose of determining their position on the surface of the earth. The moon's attraction is the principal cause of the tides, and its influence according to popular belief, unsupported, however, by scientific evidence, is strongly felt in meteorological phenomena connected with the changes of the weather. To the observer it is an unfailing source of pleasure, its closeness and exemption from an atmosphere allowing the details of its surface to be more easily seen than is the case with any of the planets, even a small telescope being sufficient to bring out well-defined images of many features.

The mean distance of the moon from the earth is 238,840 miles. Its greatest distance is 252,972 miles, and least 221,614 miles. The method of determining this has already been explained on p. 42. Its linear diameter measures 2163 miles. The moon revolves round the earth in an elliptical orbit, having the earth in one of the foci, a fact which can be verified by actual observations of its apparent diameter. When in that part of its orbit nearest the earth the moon is said to be in perigee, when farthest from the earth in apogee. At least perigean distance its apparent diameter is found to be 33′ 33″; when at greatest apogean distance it measures only 29′ 24″. It has been shown, p. 40, that the sun's apparent diameter varies from 32′ 35″ to 31′ 31′, from which it follows that the eccentricity of the earth's orbit is equal to 0·0168, or about $\frac{1}{60}$th. The variation of the moon's apparent diameter, given above, shows that the difference between the least and greatest distance of the moon from the earth is proportionally very much greater than the difference between the least and greatest distance of the earth from the sun; or, in other words, the moon's orbit about the earth is much more elliptical than the earth's orbit round the sun. The eccentricity of the lunar orbit is 0·0549, about $\frac{1}{18}$th at its mean amount, and is subject to extensive variations from the disturbing influence of the sun's attraction. The two circles in fig. 20 will convey an approximate idea of the variation of the moon's apparent diameter; the inner circle represents the diameter at greatest apogean distance, the outer circle that at least perigean distance. The orbit of the moon is inclined to the ecliptic at an angle of 5° ·9′.

In the case of the planets we have already seen the distinction which exists between their synodical and sidereal revolutions. Precisely the same distinction holds in the case of the moon's revolution about the earth. It appears to traverse the heavens in the same direction as the planets, from west to east, accomplishing a complete circuit of the heavens in 27 days 7 hours 43 minutes 11 seconds. This is the time of the moon's sidereal revolution, and its amount can be easily verified by the reader with sufficient accuracy by the following method : Watch the moon's progress in the sky till its centre comes into the same right ascension as some bright star, that is, till the star and the moon's centre are in a line with the pole of the sky. In about 27 days 8 hours resume the watch, and it will be found that the star and moon's centre are again in a line with the pole. A number of consecutive conjunctions may be observed in this way and the average taken. For example, in 1908 the star Aldebaran (α Tauri) was about 2½° south of the moon's centre, on the 14th January at 0 hours 34 minutes P.M., and again in nearly the same position on 8th March.

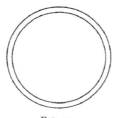

FIG. 20.

Relative apparent Diameters of the Moon at Apogee and Perigee.

Successive conjunctions of the moon and Aldebaran occurred on 4th April, 2nd and 29th May, and at regular intervals during the course of the year, up to 7th December, when a conjunction took place at 10 hours 19 minutes A.M. There are twelve such revolutions from 14th January to 7th December, covering 327 days 21 hours 45 minutes, which gives an average of 27 days 7 hours 45 minutes for the length of each sidereal revolution. This must be considered a rough verification only of the moon's sidereal period, the correct amount given above being the average resulting from many years' careful observation. At the completion of the moon's sidereal revolution the earth will have advanced over a considerable portion of its annual orbit, consequently the moon will require to move still farther in its orbit before it will come to the same relative position with respect to the sun. This, which is known as the moon's synodical period, amounts to 29 days 12 hours 44 minutes 3 seconds, and is the average time occupied in the recurrence of the successive phases of our satellite, or the period from new moon to new moon.

The variety of forms under which the moon's illuminated hemisphere, or part of it, is seen from the earth can be completely explained from the undisputed fact that it is an opaque body, shining only by reflecting the light of the sun. When it is in conjunction, or, in other words, between the earth and the sun, the whole of its illuminated hemisphere is turned away from the earth, and it is therefore invisible. This is the moment of new moon. As it moves away from the direction of the sun its bright side is turned more and more towards us. When first seen to the east of the sun it appears as a thin crescent, with its convex side towards the west, where the sun is, the horns being towards the east, the crescent increasing in breadth each day till the first quarter of a synodical revolution has been completed. Half of the enlightened hemisphere is then turned to the earth. This is the moment of first quarter. From this till it has completed half a revolution, and is seen in the part of the sky opposite to the sun, its shape is gibbous, gradually increasing to full moon. During the remaining half of the synodical revolution similar phases are shown, but in reverse order, till it again arrives at the position of conjunction with the sun. The phenomena of the moon's phases are well illustrated in fig. 6, Plate I. The inner circle of figures show the relative positions of the enlightened and dark hemispheres with reference to the sun and earth at eight separate phases of a synodical revolution. The outer figures show the appearances which the portion of the enlightened side turned to the earth present at these phases. The line which separates the bright from the dark part of the disc is known as the *terminator*. This curve, being the projection of a circle of the moon's actual surface on the apparent disc seen from the earth, is always a semi-ellipse. This fact will be recognised in the illustrations of the moon's phases in Plate IV., especially in the views of the four days' old and the five days' old moon. It will be noticed in these illustrations that the terminator is not a smooth curve. Owing to the mountainous character of the lunar surface, the tops of hills on the dark side of the terminator are illuminated by the sun's rays, while the general level of the surface around them, and the depressions near the terminator, are in darkness.

The phenomenon popularly known as the "old moon in the new moon's arms," is seen when the moon is only three or four days' old, and has still the greater portion of its dark side turned to the earth. The dark part of the disc is then faintly illuminated by light reflected to it from the earth's enlightened hemisphere, the greater portion of which is then turned towards the moon. As the bright lunar crescent increases in breadth the faint illumination is lost, partly from the increasing light of the surrounding sky, partly because the reflected "earth-shine" is lessening, as the earth's bright side is gradually being turned away from the moon.

Like the earth and the other planets the moon has a rotation on an axis, which is inclined at an angle of 83° 20′ to the plane of its orbit. The rotation is completed in exactly the same time as the revolution in its orbit about the earth, consequently it always presents the same side to the earth. If the moon's axis were absolutely perpendicular to the plane of its orbit, and if the motion in its orbit were perfectly uniform, we would see just half of the moon's surface and never any portion of the other half. From the fact that the axis is not quite perpendicular, but slightly inclined, it follows that, when the north pole leans slightly towards us, we see a little more of the region round it, and the same is the case for the south pole. Again, the irregular motion of the moon in its orbit, combined with the regular rotation on its axis, enables us sometimes to see a little farther round the western edge, sometimes a little more round the eastern. The former of these effects is known as *libration in latitude*, the latter as *libration in longitude*. There is another cause by which we are enabled to have a slightly more extended view of the moon's surface. When the moon is rising or setting it is seen not from the earth's centre, the point with reference to which it rotates uniformly on its axis, but from the extremity of a radius of the earth, or a point nearly 4000 miles away from the centre. For this reason the observer will see a little beyond the upper edge, or rather beyond what would be the upper edge if seen from the earth's centre, both at rising and setting, or more of the western edge at rising, and more of the eastern edge at setting. This is known as *diurnal libration*. These three librations combined enable us to see nearly three-fifths of the moon's complete surface.

A conspicuous feature in the movements of the moon is the difference of meridian altitude to which it attains in the course of its revolution round the earth. The orbit makes a very small angle with the ecliptic, only 5° 9'. When at new moon, or in that part of its orbit between the earth and the sun, its declination is nearly the same as that of the sun. Consequently when the noonday sun rises highest in the sky—that is, at midsummer—the *new* moon will also attain its greatest altitude. In a fortnight's time, when the moon has arrived at the *full*, or is in that part of its orbit opposite to the sun, its declination will differ from the sun's as much as possible. When the sun is in north declination the moon will be in south. Therefore the midsummer *full* moon attains only a low altitude on the meridian. In midwinter the reverse of this is the case. The sun is then in south declination, and rides low in the sky. The *new* moon is also then low in the sky, but the *full* happens now when the moon is in north declination, and attains a high altitude on the meridian.

The moon rises later each day by about an average of fifty minutes. This is due to its easterly motion amongst the stars. If we examine a calendar in which the risings and settings of the moon are given, we will find that the daily retardation of rising varies greatly. It is sometimes as much as an hour and a quarter, at other times less than half an hour. This arises from the irregular motion of the moon in its orbit, its motion eastwards being greatest when in perigee, and least when in apogee. The angle between the horizon and the ecliptic is also constantly changing, and this has also a large effect on the difference in the daily retardation. From these considerations we can arrive at the explanation of the *Harvest Moon*. It will be seen from the calendar that in each month the daily retardation of rising goes through all its variations. If the risings for several months are examined, it will be seen that the greatest or least retardation does not always correspond to the same phase of the moon. In the case of the full moon nearest to the 21st of March the daily retardations are *greater* for a few days before and after full moon than they are in the rest of the month. Again, at the full moon nearest the 23rd of September the daily retardations of rising are *less* about full moon than in the rest of the month. The September full moon, therefore, rises for several days in succession soon after sunset, and enables the agriculturist to continue the important task of gathering in his harvest after the sun has set. The reason of this will become apparent after a few minutes' study of a celestial globe. Set the globe for the latitude of the place of observation, say Edinburgh, 56° N. This is done by slipping the brass meridian round till the pole of the sky is 56° above the north horizon. Now find the sun's place amongst the stars on the 21st of March—namely, the first point of Aries, the inter-

section of the ecliptic and equator. The point exactly opposite on the globe
—viz., the opposite intersection of the ecliptic and equator—is the place of the
full moon, supposing, for the moment, that the moon moves in the ecliptic, and

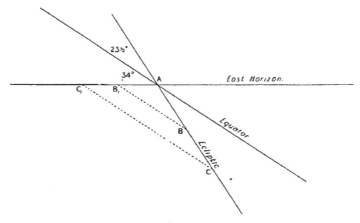

FIG. 21.

Relative positions of the Ecliptic, Equator, and East Horizon on the 21st of March.

that it is full on the day named. Bring this latter point to the eastern horizon,
and note the relative positions of the ecliptic, equator, and horizon. Looked at
from a position east of the globe, they are as in fig. 21. Now, suppose A to be

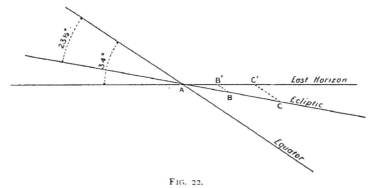

FIG. 22.

Relative positions of the Ecliptic, Equator, and East Horizon on the 23rd of September.

the point at which the full moon of 21st March rises, and let A B represent one
day's motion eastward in the ecliptic, B C the following day's motion. If the
moon rises on 21st March at 6 P.M., on the following day at 6 P.M. it will be below

the horizon at B, and will reach the horizon at B₁, moving apparently in a line parallel to the equator, some time after 6 P.M., the retardation being represented by the line B B₁. The following day it will reach the horizon along C C₁. Now consider the circumstances of the ecliptic, equator, and horizon on the 23rd of September. The sun's place in the sky is now at the other intersection of the ecliptic and equator, called the first point of Libra, and if the full moon happens on that day its place will be at the first point of Aries. Bring this point to the eastern horizon, and the relative -positions of equator, ecliptic, and horizon will be found to be as in fig. 22. Here again let A B and B C represent the daily movements of the moon in the ecliptic for the two days following the 23rd of September, and draw B B¹ and C C¹ parallel to the equator. It will be seen at once that the moon has now a much shorter space to pass over in order to reach the horizon on these days than was the case on the two days following the 21st of March. The phenomenon of the harvest moon thus depends on the fact that on the 23rd of September the ecliptic is inclined at its least angle to the eastern horizon, where the full moon is rising. If the globe be turned slowly round and the change of the inclination of the ecliptic to the eastern horizon at sunset be noted, it will be seen that this inclination is less on the day of the autumnal equinox than on any other day of the year, and that it is greatest on the day of the spring equinox. Hence the harvest moon is that full moon which occurs nearest to the 23rd of September. The fact that the moon's orbit does not coincide with the ecliptic, but is inclined to it at an angle of 5° 9′, slightly modifies the above considerations. The full moon next following the harvest moon is sometimes known as the Hunters' Moon.

The appearance of the moon's visible hemisphere to the unaided eye is too well known to need description. In the early part of the seventeenth century, when the telescope was still in its infancy, the dark patches seen on the lunar surface were denominated *seas*. Though it is now known that there is no water on the surface, and that the dark patches are certainly dry plains, the name sea is still retained for convenience.

The crater mountains are the most conspicuous peculiarity of the moon's surface. The majority of them doubtless owe their form to volcanic action, though it is probable that most of the largest craters, or walled plains, have formerly enclosed lakes of molten lava. They differ in several respects from volcanic craters on the earth. The floors are usually depressed below the surrounding surface, whereas on the earth craters are usually found on the sides or near the summits of mountains. Their numbers and dimensions also exceed enormously anything existing on the earth. As many as 33,000 have been mapped by Schmidt, of which 1000 or more have a breadth of at least nine miles. It would be impossible in a small compass to describe fully the great variety of lunar craters, from those of large dimensions, generally known as walled plains and ring mountains, to the smallest crater pits, which are to be found scattered more or less thickly over the whole surface of the moon.

Though the tendency to the circular form is the most obvious characteristic of the lunar surface, mountain chains and valleys are also to be seen. Some of the latter are of very large dimensions, others are more contracted, and may be classed as mere clefts or rills. These can be traced in some instances across plains, intersecting craters, and occasionally even traversing mountains. When the moon is full the bright streaks which radiate from a few of the craters are

E

very remarkable. The most conspicuous of them are connected with the crater known as Tycho, in the south-east quadrant. The explanation of these curious appearances is by no means certain.

The heights of many of the more prominent peaks have been measured. The earliest attempts in this direction were made by Galileo, who estimated the distance from the terminator of the isolated luminous points seen outside the bright hemisphere of the moon. These luminous points are tops of high mountains which are illuminated while the surrounding lower ground is in darkness. Galileo found that these points are sometimes distant from the terminator by an amount equal to $\frac{1}{20}$th of the moon's diameter. If P in fig. 23 be the summit of a peak, A the extremity of the terminator, and S A P a tangent to the moon's surface, S will be the direction of the sun when its rays just touch the point P. By actual measurement the value of A P can be found as a proportional part of the moon's diameter. Galileo's value, $\frac{1}{20}$th, and 2153 miles for the linear diameter of the moon, would give 5·37 miles for the height of the peak. Later measures showed that this was somewhat too great a value. Galileo's method was discarded

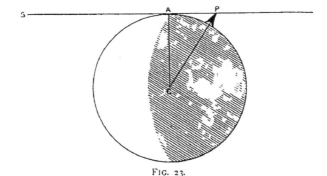

FIG. 23.

Galileo's method of measuring the height of a lunar mountain.

by more recent investigators, who have adopted the plan of measuring the actual shadow of the peak. This can be much more accurately done, because lunar shadows are sharp and well defined, owing to the absence of an atmosphere The altitude of the sun above the horizon of the point of the moon's surface under measurement must be taken into consideration in this method, because on this depends the length of the shadow at the moment. At the actual terminator the sun's rays are horizontal, and at the centre of the enlightened hemisphere they are vertical. Hence, near the terminator the shadows are long, and near the centre of the bright hemisphere they disappear altogether. The sun's altitude depends on the position of the peak with reference to the terminator. In this way Messrs Beer and Mädler have measured the heights of over 800 peaks; of these they found several to exceed three miles in elevation. The height of Mont Blanc above the sea-level is 15,760 feet, or almost exactly 3 miles. The diameters of many of the circular craters have also been measured. The crater called Newton, situated near the south pole, is probably the deepest on the moon's surface. The highest peak on its walls rises to 23,900 feet above the interior, or about $4\frac{1}{2}$ miles. The

Dörfel Mountains, also near the south pole, and close to the edge of the visible hemisphere, are seen in profile in favourable conditions of libration One peak rises to 26,000 feet above the level of the edge, or nearly five miles.

The nomenclature of the lunar formations is originally due to Riccioli, an astronomer of Boulogne, who, in 1651, published a map in which he affixed the names of distinguished astronomers and mathematicians to the more prominent features of the surface, except to the grey plains, which had already been called seas by Hevelius of Dantzic. This system is still adhered to, and many names have been added in modern times.

Figures 24 to 31 show a few of the most interesting portions of the moon's surface. They have been reproduced by kind permission of MM. Loewy and Puiseux from photographs taken by them with the great equatorial of the Paris Observatory. The craters and other features shown may be identified by aid of the small reference letters placed along the side and at the top of each of the pictures. The following table gives the names of the chief features shown in each Plate, and the reference letters by which they can be identified :—

Fig. 24.—South Pole	Fig. 28.—*a.* Copernicus
a. Clavius	*b.* Eratosthenes
b. Longomontanus	
c. Scheiner	
Fig. 25.—*a.* Clavius	Fig. 29.—Apennines
b. Tycho	*a.* Archimedes
c. Longomontanus	*b.* Sinus Æstuum
d. Maginus	*c.* Aristillus
Fig. 26.—*a.* Maurolycus	Fig. 30.—Mare Imbrium
b. Stöfler	*a.* Plato
c. Walter	*b.* Sinus Iridum
Fig. 27.—*a.* Arzachel	Fig. 31.—*a.* Cassini
b. Alphonsus	*b.* Eudoxus
c. Ptolemy	*c.* Aristoteles
d. Albategnius	*d.* Valley of the Alps.

The figures show the portions of the lunar surface as seen in an inverting telescope. Hence it must be borne in mind that the top of each picture is south, the bottom north, the right hand side is east, and the left side west. In this sense the points of the compass are referred to in the descriptions which follow. Many of the facts and most of the dimensions have been taken from Neison's *Moon*, some also from Webb's *Celestial Objects for Common Telescopes*—works which no student of Selenography should be without.

For convenience the visible surface is usually divided into four quadrants by two lines at right angles, one from north to south, the other from east to west, through the centre of the moon's disc. The quadrants so formed are named the north-west, north-east, south-east, and south-west quadrants.

Fig. 24 shows the South Pole and part of the south-east quadrant. The walled plain Clavius is one of the largest on the moon's surface, being 142 miles in diameter. Its walls are exceedingly high and steep, one of the peaks on the western side measuring 17,300 feet above the floor. A large number of small craters can be seen scattered along the wall and interior surface. Two of those on the western wall are of fairly large proportions, the ring of one rising as high as 11,700 feet above its floor. Towards the centre of Clavius is a crater

FIG. 24.

South Pole ; *a*, Clavius ; *b*, Longomontanus ; *c*, Scheiner.

of 16 miles in diameter. Its walls rise 2910 feet above the floor of Clavius, and 9362 feet above its own interior surface. Hence the floor of this comparatively small formation is 6452 feet lower than the plain in which it has been formed, and 23,750 feet below the top of the great peak on the western wall. Clavius should be observed when the sun is rising or setting on that part of the moon's surface. The photograph was taken when the moon was twenty-two and

a half days old, and the terminator had reached the western wall on the outside.
At sunrise the peaks first, then the walls are illuminated.   While the interior is
still dark it looks like a great bay opening out of the dark side of the terminator,
and perceptibly blunting the southern horn to the naked eye.

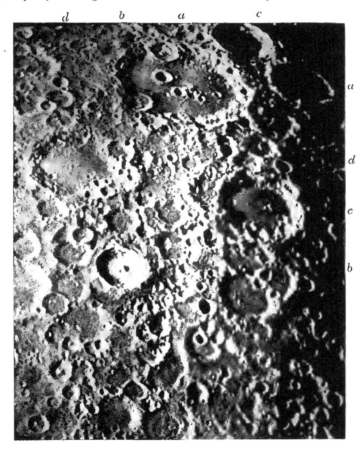

FIG. 25.

a, Clavius ; *b*, Tycho ; *c*, Longomontanus ; *d*. Maginus.

Longomontanus is 90 miles in diameter and very deep, and has on its west
wall a peak 14,500 feet above the interior.   On the floor are several craters and
craterlets, collected chiefly in groups at the foot of the walls.   Longomontanus
is surrounded by a rugged region of mountain ravines dotted with innumerable
craters.   Scheiner is a walled plain of somewhat smaller dimensions than the
other two in the figure.   It is 70 miles in diameter.   In the centre of the

floor a bright crater is distinctly seen.   South of the line joining Clavius and
Scheiner is Blancanus, a fine ring plain with lofty walls.

Figure 25 covers partly the same ground as figure 24, but is taken under
different illumination, as will be seen by the shadows.   It includes also Maginus

FIG. 26.

a, Maurolycus ; *b*, Stöfler ; *c*, Walter.

and the great crater Tycho.   The sun has just risen on Longomontanus, and
Clavius is well illuminated.   The floors of Scheiner and Blancanus are shown
still in shade, though their walls are partly illuminated.   The moon was ten
days old when this photograph was taken.

Tycho is probably the most conspicuous object on the moon's surface.
It is a great crater plain with a broad circular wall, built up of numerous

terraces outside and inside. The wall rises to 17,000 feet above the floor. It has a central mountain between 5000 and 6000 feet high, surrounded by a mountainous mass of less elevation. On the exterior wall numerous terraces can be traced, which give place outside their base to an irregular confused

FIG. 27.

a, Arzachel; *b*, Alphonsus; *c*, Ptolemy; *d*, Albategnius.

mass of mountains and craters. The principal streak system radiates from Tycho as a centre, and stretches over nearly a fourth of the visible surface of the moon. Towards the south they reach the edge, but their longest visible extension is to the north-west, where they reach the *Mare Serenitatis*, crossing nearly the whole disc of the moon. *Maginus*, also shown in this figure, has been described as the ruins of a magnificent walled plain. The surrounding walls remain perfect only at a few points, the rest of the border being a mass of mountain ranges and groups of peaks.

In figure 26 are shown three great walled plains—Maurolycus, Stöfler, and Walter. The wall of Maurolycus rises at one point to 13,800 feet above the interior, and is split up by numerous valleys and ridges, broken into by several craters and crater pits. On the south wall there is a great crater plain, on the north-east there is another shallow ring plain with a deep crater on its floor. On the floor of Maurolycus can be seen two crater pits and a mountainous mass. Maurolycus and Stöfler are both rendered nearly invisible at full moon by the bright streaks radiating from Tycho.

Stöfler is surrounded on the east by a wall rising in places from 10,000 to 11,000 feet. On the west the wall is broken by the great ring plain Faraday. On the north wall are a number of crater formations, and a break in the wall appears to connect Stöfler with the large walled plain Fernelius. Farther north is a smaller ring plain called Nonius.

Walter is surrounded by mountain chains, in which are a large number of separate peaks, one on the north-east side rising nearly 10,000 feet above the interior. The walls are intersected by valleys and ravines. A central peak rises nearly 5000 feet above the floor.

In figure 27, Ptolemy, Alphonsus, and Arzachel form a chain of great walled plains, lying north and south. The north and largest is Ptolemy, with a diameter of 115 miles. On its interior surface may be seen a bright and deep crater to the west of the centre. The walls consist of high mountains of irregular formation, and at the south side it is crossed by rugged passes, opening into the plain of Alphonsus. Several peaks on the east and north walls have been measured, and found to range from 2500 to 6000 feet above the interior.

Alphonsus, the second of these walled plains, is 83 miles in diameter, and is surrounded by high terraced walls, rising in great peaks, one 7000, another 5500 feet above the interior plain. Many long valleys are noticeable, and at the foot of the east wall there is a dark patch which can be seen in full moon on an apparently level surface.

Arzachel lies south of Alphonsus, and is about 65 miles in diameter, and is much more regular than either Alphonsus or Ptolemy. Its walls abound in terraces and valleys. The western wall rises at one point to 13,500 feet, at another to nearly 9000 feet above the interior. The eastern wall is fully 10,000 feet above the interior, though only 6000 above the outer surface. Near the centre is a peak rising 5000 feet, and west of it a deep crater.

Albategnius is 64 miles in diameter, and has a central peak over 4000 feet high. The surrounding wall is much broken up by the formation of crater-like depressions. On the east side is a fine ring plain with a central peak.

Figure 28 is a view of the great ring plain Copernicus and its surroundings. Copernicus is 56 miles in diameter, and with its terraced walls and central peaks forms one of the most perfect specimens of crater formation on the lunar surface. The walls are very broad, and rise into peaks separated by depressions at nearly regular intervals round its ring. The central mountain mass is divided into several peaks, three of which are conspicuous. North of Copernicus lie the Carpathian Mountains. Between Copernicus and Eratosthenes will be seen a curious row of small crater pits, while traces of numberless still smaller formations crowd the whole region. Copernicus is the centre of a system of light streaks, which, like those radiating from Tycho, are only seen under vertical illumination. Eratosthenes is a very perfect crater ring of 37 miles diameter, with a conspicuous central mountain

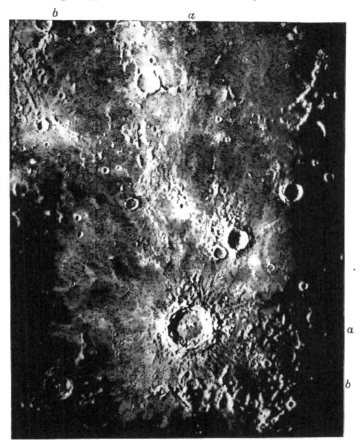

FIG. 28.

a, Copernicus ; *b*, Eratosthenes.

divided into several peaks. A little south of the line joining the crater with Copernicus lies Stadius, an almost obliterated ring, remnants of which are, however, well shown in the photograph. The two rings are connected by a chain of mountains reaching 4500 feet elevation. West of these craters lies the *Sinus Æstuum*, a region almost devoid of craters, and presenting a remarkable contrast to the district between Copernicus and Eratosthenes, which has been compared to a sieve, so abundant are the crater pits which it contains.

Figure 29 shows the lunar Apennines, a tremendous chain of mountain masses. On the south-west it slopes gradually to the general level of the

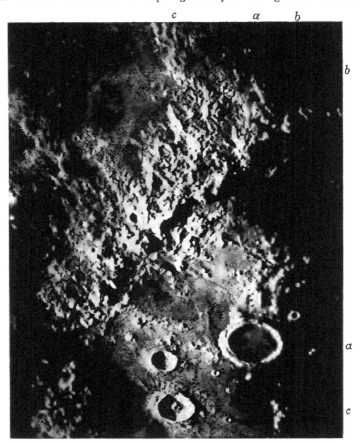

FIG. 29.

Apennines; *a*, Archimedes; *b*, Sinus Æstuum; *c*, Aristillus.

surface. On the north-east the whole chain presents a line of stupendous precipices. The highest point, almost south of Archimedes, rises to an elevation of 18,000 feet. About first quarter, when the range is coming into sunshine, the bright tops of the peaks can be seen outside the terminator with the naked eye. The photograph was taken when the moon was eight days old.

Archimedes is a walled plain of 50 miles diameter, with a smooth interior surface, which shows no trace of any mountains or peaks on it. The exterior wall is much terraced, and south of it is a rugged region of mountain chains and valleys.

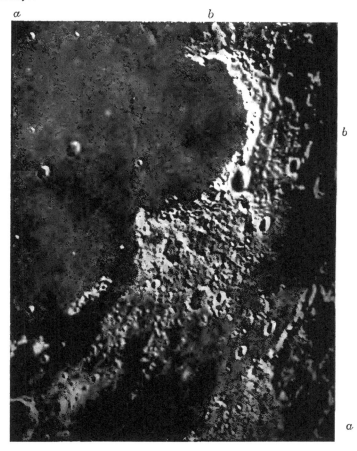

a   b

b

a

FIG. 30.

Mare Imbrium ; *a*, Plato ; *b*, Sinus Iridum.

Aristillus is one of the most perfectly formed craters on the moon's surface. It is 34 miles in diameter, and its wall rises in one place to 11,000, another to 8800 feet above the interior, which is some 3000 feet lower than the surface outside the wall. Ridges and mountain chains radiate in all directions from this crater, and connect it on the south with Autolycus, a very similar but smaller crater, 23 miles in diameter, and with a central mountain by no means so distinct as that of Aristillus. Part of the *Sinus Æstuum* appears at the south-east corner of this photograph, while along the rest of the east side lies the *Mare Imbrium*, the largest of the grey plains so conspicuous to the naked eye. On the western side appears a small portion of the *Mare*

FIG. 31.

a, Cassini; *b*, Eudoxus; *c*, Aristoteles; *d*, Valley of the Alps.

Serenitatis. The central meridian of the moon's visible surface passes between Archimedes and the two neighbouring craters, Aristillus and Autolycus, and the region shown in this photograph lies about half way between the equator and north pole; from which it is easy to locate with the naked eye the positions of the two grey plains referred to.

Figure 30 shows a portion of the *Mare Imbrium* farther to the north than the region shown in figure 29, with the great bay known as *Sinus Iridum* opening out of it. Within the bay the surface is of remarkable smoothness, while just outside the line joining the promontories, which are about 140 miles apart, a few slight ridges may be seen wrinkling a surface on which no other feature is visible, with the exception of an occasional small crater. The bay is encompassed by colossal cliffs, the western limit of a rugged mass of mountains, the summits of which rise to 15,000 feet and 12,000 feet at two points near the south-eastern promontory. The very numerous summits are intersected by a perfect network of valleys and ravines, with several conspicuous craters. The mountain chain runs in a north-west direction to the crater Plato, which is partly shown in the figure.

Plato has a level interior surface 60 miles in diameter. It lies near the north edge of the moon and close to the central meridian. Under different conditions of libration its distance from the edge appears to change, being in the extreme of north libration only half distance it is in south libration.

Figure 31 shows a portion of the moon's surface lying west of that in figure 30. The Valley of the Alps is a very curious formation. It is 83 miles long and from 4 to 6 miles broad, and traverses the whole range of the Alpine Highlands like a great cleft. South of the Alps lies the ring plain Cassini, showing a large and conspicuous crater near the centre of its floor, and a second smaller one under the south-east wall. West of Cassini is the highest portion of the Caucasus Mountains, whose rugged hills are much intersected by long valleys and depressions. The large crater lying almost in the centre of the mountain mass is *Calippus*, and east of it is a peak 18,500 feet high. Several other peaks in this neighbourhood are above 10,000 feet elevation.

Aristoteles and Eudoxus are a magnificent pair of ring craters, the former about 50 miles in diameter, and with two peaks on its east and west wall rising over 10,000 feet above the interior. Eudoxus is rather less in diameter, but has somewhat loftier peaks on its wall. The two craters shown partly illuminated in the south-east corner of this figure are Aristillus and Autolycus, shown also on figure 29 in higher light.

Plate IV. exhibits several views of the moon's surface. In the upper corner, to the left, is a representation of the crater Copernicus, from an original drawing by Padre Secchi. In the upper right-hand corner is a view of the moon twenty days old, reduced from a photograph by MM. Lœwy and Puiseux. In the centre is a view of the full moon, from a drawing by Bode. Tycho, near the upper part of the disc, and Copernicus are well seen in the centres of the two conspicuous streak systems, and many of the other features referred to above can be identified. The remaining figures in the Plate indicate the general appearance of the moon in various stages of illumination.

CHAPTER XI.

AN eclipse of the sun takes place when, the moon being new, its opaque body intervenes between the earth and sun, thus shutting off the light of the sun from a portion of the earth's surface. An eclipse of the moon, on the other hand, takes place when, the moon being full, and the earth between the sun and moon, the latter becomes involved in the shadow cast by the earth. The earth and moon being spherical bodies, and the sun of much larger dimensions than either, the true shadows or umbræ cast by them must be conical in shape. This cone of deep shadow will be surrounded by a region of partial shadow or penumbra, from which the sun's light is only partly intercepted. This is evident from the figures on Plates V. and VI., which are intended to show only the method of formation of the umbra and penumbra. Their proper proportions could not be represented distinctly in the space available, both umbra and penumbra being very much longer and narrower than they appear in the figures. Mention has been made of the apparent diameters of the sun and moon, and attention has been called to the fact that both these quantities vary. The moon's apparent diameter varies much more than the sun's, the former from 33′ 31″ to 29′ 22″, and the latter from 32′ 35″ to 31′ 30″. On the variation of these quantities, and on another circumstance which will be noted presently, depend the different types of eclipses. Solar eclipses are of three types—total, annular, and partial ; lunar are either total or partial. It will be seen that the average apparent diameters of sun and moon do not differ very greatly, for though the sun is of enormously greater absolute dimensions than the moon, its distance from the earth is also greater in about the same proportion.

If the moon, in the course of its monthly revolution round the earth, revolved in an orbit which coincided with the ecliptic, that is, with the plane of the earth's orbit about the sun, the centres of the moon, earth, and sun would then always lie in the same plane, and at every revolution the moon, when in conjunction, would come exactly between the sun and earth, and there would be a solar eclipse once a month. In a fortnight, when the moon came round to the opposite side of the earth, there would also be a lunar eclipse. The moon's orbit is, however, inclined to the ecliptic at a small angle, 5° 9″, and consequently the moon does not pass every month when in conjunction exactly between the earth and sun, but usually somewhat above or below the line joining their centres. At opposition it will also pass as a rule somewhat above or below this line. An eclipse will not take place unless the moon, when in conjunction or opposition, is also near one of its nodes, the points at which its orbit intersects the ecliptic. Hence arises the name ecliptic, the plane in or near which the moon must be in order that an eclipse may take place. Whether an eclipse of the sun will then be total or annular depends on the length of the shadow of the moon and the distance of the moon from its node. Plate V., fig. 7, illustrates the circumstances of a total solar eclipse, showing the moon's shadow in contact with the earth's surface. In this case a total eclipse is seen from those parts of the earth which are traversed by the shadow, and a partial eclipse at places involved in the penumbra. The shadow moves from west to east tracing out a band on the earth's surface which can never exceed 190 miles in breadth. The motion of the shadow with reference to the earth's surface is compounded of three movements, those of the moon and the earth in their orbits, and of the earth's rotation on its axis, the resultant movement is always as stated from west to east. The manner in which the varying length of the shadow and the distance of the moon from the earth alter the conditions of an eclipse will appear more clear on reference to fig. 32, where A is the apex of the moon's conical shadow. The lines A B and A C drawn touching the moon's edge also touch the edges of the sun, and the spectator at A sees the moon exactly between his eyes and the sun, and covering the whole of the sun's disc. In this case there would be a total eclipse, but of momentary duration. If, now, the eye be moved to E^1, nearer to the moon

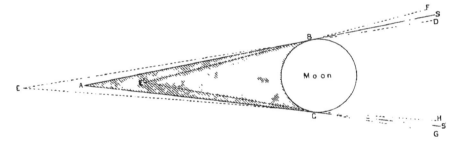

FIG. 32.

than the apex of the shadow, the moon will be seen under a greater angle, and will totally eclipse the sun and a ring of sky around it for an appreciable time. Plate V., fig. 8, illustrates an annular eclipse, from which it will be seen that in this type of eclipse the apex of the shadow does not reach the earth. The spectator is, therefore, farther from the moon, as at E in fig. 32, and sees the moon under a smaller angle than the sun along the dotted lines E D and E H. The moon is thus seen projected on the sun's disc, with a ring of bright sun around it. The average length of the shadow may be determined as follows : Let S in fig. 33 be the centre of the sun, M that of the moon, and P the apex of the shadow. We know that the proportion between S S^1, the radius of the sun, and M M^1, the radius of the moon, is the same as that between P S and P M. From which it follows that the difference between these radii bears the same proportion to the moon's radius as the difference between P S and P M, which is S M, bears to P M, the length of the shadow. The sun's radius is 433,180 miles, the moon's 1080 miles, the difference = 432,100. Again S M is equal to the difference between the sun's distance and the moon's distance from the earth ; that is, the difference between 92,897,000 miles and 238,840 miles, the average difference = 92,658,160 miles. Hence we have the following sum in the rule of three—432,100 : 1080 :: 92,658,160 :

the length of the shadow, measured from the centre of the moon to the apex. This gives the length of the shadow under average conditions as 231,592 miles. But the average distance of the moon from the earth, as stated above, is 238,840 miles ; therefore under average conditions the moon's shadow would not reach the earth, and an annular eclipse only would be possible. As the distance between the sun and the moon in conjunction varies, so the length of the shadow varies also. When this distance is greater than the average the shadow is of course

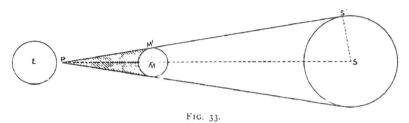

FIG. 33.

longer, and in fact it becomes long enough to reach the earth and make a total eclipse possible.

Similarly, a lunar eclipse in the true shadow would be impossible if the earth's shadow were not long enough to reach the moon in opposition. We can determine the length of the earth's shadow as follows: In this case, fig. 34, the radius of the sun is to the radius of the earth in the same proportion as the distance P S of the sun's centre from the apex of the shadow is to the distance of the earth's centre from the apex ; or the difference of S S¹ and E E¹ is to E E¹

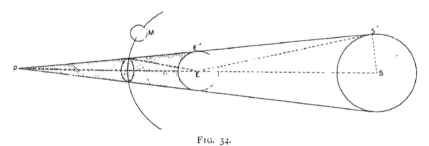

FIG. 34.

as S E to E P ; the latter being the length of the shadow measured from the earth's centre to the apex. Hence we have 429,217 : 3964 :: 92,897,000 : length of shadow. From this the length of the shadow comes out 863,840 miles, or about three and a half times as long as the distance of the moon from the earth. Though this amount varies it does not vary so much as to make the shadow ever less than the distance of the moon. A total lunar eclipse would thus be inevitable every month if the moon's orbit were in the ecliptic, provided the section of the shadow through which the moon passed were of sufficient breadth to cover the moon, or in other words, if the section of the shadow subtended a greater angle at the earth than the moon did. It can easily be ascertained that the section is about two and a half times as broad as the moon's disc, and is never less than twice as broad.[1] From this fact it follows that an annular eclipse of the moon is impossible.

The possibility of the occurrence of eclipses, either solar or lunar, depends on the distance of the moon when new or full from the nodes of its orbit. If it is actually at the node, or within a very short distance of it when new, an eclipse of the sun either total or annular must take place. At a somewhat greater distance from the node a partial eclipse only is possible, and still farther away neither is possible. If, in the fig. 35, N C be in the plane of the ecliptic, and N M the moon's orbit, N the node, M, M₁, M₂, and N different positions of the new moon in its orbit, and S, S₁, S, and N corresponding positions of the sun, when the moon is new at the point M no eclipse will take place, but the moon's edge will just come into contact with the edge of the sun. At M₁ and M partial eclipses take place, and at the actual node itself the eclipse will be central, and either total or annular according to the length of the moon's shadow under the particular circumstances of the eclipse. The distance from the node at which the moon must be in order that the discs of sun and moon may just touch under average con-

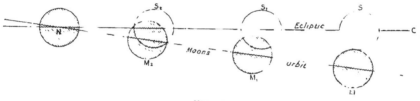

FIG. 35.

ditions is 18° on either side of the node, or 36' in all. This is known as the solar ecliptic limit, and the line joining the two points at which the moon's orbit intersects the ecliptic must point within 18° of the sun in order that an eclipse of the sun may take place. Now, the sun moves round the ecliptic the whole 360° of the circle in 365¼ days, hence it moves to the east over the 36° in about 36½ days, and supposing it to be just outside the western extremity of the ecliptic limit at any new new moon, at the next, or in 29½ days, it cannot have moved east far enough to escape eclipse. It follows that at least one eclipse of the sun must take place at each of the moon's nodes, or two each year. They may, however, be only partial eclipses. Again, if the moon is new when just within the ecliptic limit west of the node, there will be a partial solar eclipse then, and another may take place at next new moon. Two partial eclipses may similarly take place when the sun is opposite the other node. If the first pair occur as early as possible in January there may be a fifth solar eclipse in December, owing to the westward movement of the moon's nodes bringing the sun to the node earlier each year. There may, therefore, be five solar eclipses in a calendar year.

---

[1] It will easily be seen from fig. 34 that if e be the semi-angle subtended at the earth's centre by the section of the shadow, $e = p + p^1 - s$, when p and p^1 are the horizontal parallaxes of the sun and moon, and s the sun's angular semi-diameter. Hence under average conditions $e = 8.80'' + 57' 2.2'' - 16' 2'' = 41' 9 0''$. The angle e varies from about 38' to 45'.

F

The lunar ecliptic limits will be readily understood from fig. 2, Plate VI. If the moon be full in the position to the left of the illustration no eclipse will take place. In this position, however, the moon will be within the penumbral shadow, not shown in the figure. A partial eclipse and a total eclipse at the node are also shown. The lunar ecliptic limit, or the distance from the nodes at which the moon must be just to touch the edge of the earth's true shadow, is about $12\frac{1}{2}°$ on each side of the node, under average circumstance of the relative distances of earth, moon, or sun ; or $25°$ along the ecliptic. As the sun traverses this amount in about twenty-six days, there can be but one lunar eclipse at each node, or two in the year. There may thus be seven eclipses, lunar and solar

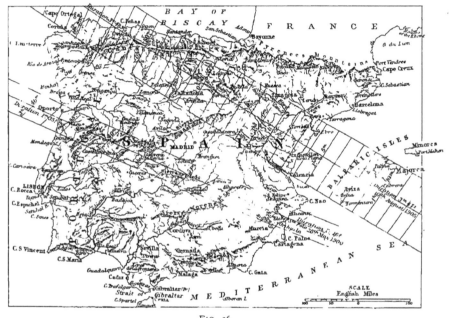

FIG. 36.

Tracks of the Total Solar Eclipses of 1900 and 1905 across Spain.

together, in a calendar year. This is the greatest possible number, and it occurs only at long intervals.

From the relative lengths of the solar and lunar ecliptic limits, $36°$ and $25°$ respectively, it will be seen that the chance of the occurrence of a solar eclipse is greater than that of a lunar eclipse. In fact, they occur in the proportion of nearly four solar to three lunar. This refers to all types of eclipses as seen from any point of the earth's surface. Lunar eclipses are, however, seen from any point of a hemisphere of the earth's surface, or rather, more owing to the earth's rotation during the progress of the eclipse. Solar eclipses when total, on the other hand, are visible only from a comparatively narrow band traced out by the motion of the shadow in the time of eclipse; when annular, they are seen as such from a similar band of the earth's surface; as partial eclipses they are seen from a more extended area, but not from a complete hemisphere. It results that lunar eclipses are more frequently seen from any particular locality than solar eclipses are.

Fig. 36 has been reproduced from a map published by the Spanish Government showing the paths of the total eclipses of 1900 and 1905 across Spain. The path of the moon's shadow in each eclipse is marked by three lines, the middle one showing all places from which the eclipse is seen, not only as total but central, and therefore of longest duration. The outer lines show the limits beyond which the eclipse will not be total, but partial only. The duration of totality on the central line, and the time of the middle of the eclipse at different localities are marked at intervals along the lines.

Previous to the middle of the nineteenth century the value of astronomical observations of all kinds of eclipses lay chiefly in noting the exact times and circumstances of the various phases, for the purpose of improving our knowledge of the complicated theory of the moon's motion, so as to facilitate the construction of tables by which future eclipses might be predicted with even greater accuracy than had previously been possible. In recent years, whenever an opportunity has presented itself, observations have been made of the occultations of groups of small stars during a total or nearly total eclipse of the moon. When the moon is uneclipsed, owing to the brightness of its light, occulations of stars down to about the sixth magnitude only can be observed with advantage. When, however, the eclipsed moon happens to occult a number of stars, a whole series of observations can be obtained at a number of distant observatories, the combination of which gives a much more valuable result than a few isolated observations could possibly do, and enables the moon's place in the sky, as well as its size and distance, to be determined with greatly increased accuracy.

To investigators of the physical constitution of the sun, the total solar eclipse is of vastly greater interest and importance than any other eclipse. On these occasions, rare and of short duration, the opaque body of the moon, interposed between the sun and the observer's eye, acts as a screen, cutting off the superabundant brilliance of the sun's rays, and enabling him to observe those phenomena of the sun's atmosphere which reach outside the edge of the moon's disc.

From the illustration of a total solar eclipse in fig. 7, Plate V., it will be seen that the section of the moon's shadow where it reaches the earth's surface is of comparatively small diameter. Its average breadth is about 90 miles, and may be as much as 180 miles. It moves at an average rate of over 1000 miles an hour. Hence the duration of totality at any point can never be greater than seven and a half minutes, and is usually much less.

The SAROS, which was discovered by the Chaldeans seven centuries before the Christian era, is a cycle of 18 years 11⅓ days, after which a regular recurrence of eclipses takes place in similar order, and of nearly similar type, to those which occurred in the preceding cycle. It has been already remarked that the occurrence of eclipses depends on the position of the moon at new and full with respect to the nodes, or points in which its orbits cuts the ecliptic. If, therefore, the line joining the nodes always remained stationary, pointing to the same part of the zodiac, eclipses would always happen about the same two dates every year, namely, about the months when the sun would be close to the two opposite signs of the zodiac to which the line of nodes pointed. The line of nodes is not, however, stationary, but has a retrograde motion in the ecliptic of 3′ 10·64″ per day. The nodes, therefore, move round the ecliptic in the same direction as the hands of a watch, making a complete revolution in 18 years 218 days 21 hours. In each of the four figures annexed the outer circle represents the ecliptic, and the moon's orbit is shown inclined to it, the broken curve in each case being that half of the orbit which is below or to the south of the ecliptic, the unbroken curve being the half orbit above, or to the north of the ecliptic; A is thus the ascending node, D the descending. The first figure shows the line of nodes directed to the opposite signs Aries and Libra. So long as the nodes remained in this position eclipses could only happen in March-April, when the sun is in or near Aries, or in September-October, when it is in Libra. In one-fourth of the above period of revolution, the nodes will have moved in the direction of the short arrows, and will be in Capricornus and Cancer. In the third figure they are again pointing to Aries

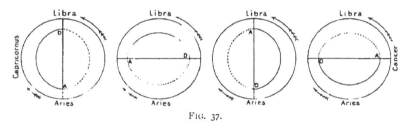

FIG. 37.

and Libra, but the ascending and descending nodes have changed places. In two similar quarter revolutions the nodes will have returned to their original position. As the sun's apparent motion in the ecliptic is in the direction of the large arrows, it will arrive at the place of the moon's nodes earlier each year, and eclipses will happen also earlier each year. Thus the dates of the eclipses of the sun in 1907 were 14th January and 10th July, whereas in 1908 they occured on 3rd January and 28th June, the earlier eclipse in each of these years happening when the sun was opposite the moon's ascending node, the later ones when it was opposite the descending. The time the sun takes after passing one of the moon's nodes to meet the same node again can be found by dividing the whole circle of the ecliptic, or 360°, into two parts proportional to the rates at which the sun and the node respectively traverse the ecliptic, that is, in the proportion of 59′ 8″ to 3′ 10·64″, their average daily movements. From this it appears that the sun meets the node again after traversing 341·63° of the ecliptic, which it does in 346·63 days. The moon similarly meets the same node of its orbit in a period which is less than a complete sidereal revolution. This period amounts to 27 days 5 hours 5 minutes 36 seconds, or 27·212 days. These two periods, as well as the moon's synodical revolution, or time between one new moon and the next, are concerned in the occurrence of eclipses. The Chaldeans discovered that (a) 242 nodical revolutions of the moon, (*b*) 223 synodical revolutions, and (*c*) nineteen returns of the sun to the same lunar node were all nearly equal. Thus:—

(*a*) 27·212   days × 242 = 6585·304 days
(*b*) 29·5306 days × 223 = 6585·324 days
(*c*) 346·63   days × 19 = 6585·970 days

Hence after 6585$\frac{1}{3}$ days, or 18 years 11$\frac{1}{3}$ days, the moon will be at the same position with respect to the nodes, and also with respect to new and full; and the sun will be within less than one degree of the same position with respect to the node. The sun, moon, and moon's nodes, therefore, repeat their movements and relative positions after the lapse of this time, causing a recurrence of the cycle of eclipses. As an example, in 1883 there was a total solar eclipse on 6th May at 9 hours 45 minutes P.M., and also an annular eclipse on 30th October at 11 hours 36 minutes P.M. Adding to these dates 18 years 11$\frac{1}{3}$ days we arrive at 1901, 18th May, 5 hours 29 minutes A.M., and 11th November, 7 hours 18 minutes A.M., when total and annular eclipses of the sun took place. The effect of a fraction of a day, not quite one-third, is to alter the hour at which the eclipses happen, or, in other words, to make them visible from different parts of the earth. By this cycle the Chaldeans were enabled to predict both solar and lunar eclipses with considerable accuracy.

CHAPTER XII.

GENERAL SURVEY OF THE PLANETARY SYSTEM.

THE Planetary System as at present known consists of eight principal planets, viz., Mercury, Venus, the Earth, Mars, Jupiter, Saturn, Uranus, and Neptune, besides the group of minor planets revolving round the sun in orbits lying between those of Mars and Jupiter, of which about 600 are known to exist, the number being every year increased by new discoveries. The satellites by which several of the principal planets are attended must also be included. Thus, the Earth is accompanied by one satellite, Mars by two, Jupiter by seven, Saturn by ten, Uranus by four, and Neptune by one. The aggregate number of satellites at present known amounts, therefore, to twenty-five.

The planets may conveniently be divided into three classes: First, the four interior planets, Mercury, Venus, the Earth, and Mars, all of which are of moderate dimensions and nearly equal in density; second, the group of minor planets, all of which are small and revolve within a comparatively narrow zone of the planetary regions; third, the four exterior planets, which are distinguished by their immense magnitude, by their moderate density, and by the circumstance that they are each accompanied by one or more satellites. The number of satellites attending the four outer planets is twenty-two out of the twenty-five known to exist. Views of the planetary system are given on Plate VII.

MERCURY, when favourably situated for observation, may be seen with the naked eye shining as a brilliant star sometimes in the west a little after sunset, at other times in the east a little before sunrise. It is most favourably situated at those greatest elongations when the ecliptic makes a large angle with the horizon. Thus in August, September, and October it should be looked for before sunrise about the dates of its greatest elongation west; on the other hand, in February, March, and April, Mercury will be most easily seen after sunset, about the dates of its greatest eastern elongation.

The mean distance of Mercury from the sun is 36,000,000 miles. Its orbit is, however, very eccentric, and its real distance is therefore subject to great variation in the course of a revolution. The eccentricity is about one-fifth, and the variation of distance amounts to 15,000,000 miles, its perihelion, or least distance from the sun, being 28,500,000, and its aphelion, or greatest distance, 43,500,000 miles. The greatest distance of this planet from the earth 133,000,000 miles, and the least 58,000,000. Its least and greatest apparent diameters are 4·5″ and 12·5″ respectively. Its real diameter is 2960 miles. Viewed with a telescope, Mercury exhibits phases like those of Venus, or the moon, depending on its position relatively to the earth and sun. This proves that it is an opaque body like the earth, shining only by the reflected light of the sun.

As Mercury revolves round the sun in an orbit which is within the earth's orbit, it would pass exactly between the earth and the sun and appear as a black spot on the sun's disc every synodical revolution, if its orbit were in the plane of the ecliptic. Since, however, its orbit is inclined to the ecliptic at an angle of $7°$, it is only when the planet is' at or near one of the nodes of its orbit that such a transit across the sun's disc can take place. Transits of Mercury can happen only in May or November, because in these months the line drawn from the sun's centre to the earth passes through the nodes of Mercury's orbit. They occur at intervals ranging from three and a half to thirteen years. The French astronomer Gassendi, in 1631, was the first to observe Mercury crossing the sun's disc. Plate VIII. contains a representation of the apparent paths of the planet over the sun's disc during the twentieth century. As transits both of Mercury and Venus occur when these planets are at inferior conjunction, their apparent movements in the sky are then retrograde, or from east to west, consequently transits begin on the east side of the sun's disc.

The time of the rotation of a planet on its axis is determined by observation of some inequality or marking on its surface. Near the beginning of the nineteenth century Schröter, an astronomer renowned, amongst other work, for his telescopic study of the planets, observed that one of the horns of the crescent of Mercury showed an irregular marking at certain intervals. From repeated observation of these intervals he found a period of rotation of 24 hours 5 minutes. A similar series of observations of Venus gave for that planet a rotation period of 23 hours 21 minutes. These markings on the discs of Mercury and Venus are so indistinct that the rotation periods determined from them are considered doubtful, and they have accordingly been so marked in Plate VII. Recently Schiaparelli of Milan, after a lengthened study of the two planets, announced that they both rotate on their axis in the same time as they revolve round the sun. They would, therefore, always present the same side to the sun. Though these results are open to the same objection as Schröter's from the indistinctness of the markings, there are reasons for considering them more likely to be true than the older determinations. M. Belopolski of Pulkowa Observatory has, however, found from spectroscopic observations of Venus, made in 1900, a rotation period of about 24 hours.

VENUS is the most brilliant of all the planets. Its mean distance from the sun is 67,000,000 miles. The orbit of the planet is only slightly elliptical, the eccentricity being $\frac{1}{147}$th. The variation of its distance from the sun is, therefore, inconsiderable, amounting only to about 1,000,000 miles. Its distance from the earth, however, varies from a maximum of 160,000,000 miles at superior conjunction to a minimum of about 26,000,000 at inferior conjunction. The real diameter of Venus is 7600 miles.

One of the first fruits of Galileo's application of the telescope to astronomical observation consisted in his discovery of the fact that Venus exhibits phases like the moon. This proved that the planet is seen by sunlight reflected by it to the earth, and so far supplied a strong confirmation of the Copernican system of the universe, inasmuch as the phases could be explained only on the supposition that Venus revolved in an orbit round the sun.

The transits of Venus across the sun's disc have already been referred to, p. 44, in connection with the determination of the earth's distance from the sun.

They can occur only in June and December, because the earth is in these months in a line with one or other of the nodes of Venus' orbit and the sun. They take place in pairs, between the first and second of which there is an interval of eight years. The interval between one pair and the next is 121½ and 105½ years alternately. Illustrations of the pair of transits which occurred in December of 1874 and 1882 are given in Plate VIII., accompanied in each case with a view of the illuminated hemisphere of the earth at the ingress and egress of the planet. The next pair will take place in the years 2004 and 2012 in the month of June.

The next planet in order of distance from the sun is the EARTH. Its mean distance from the sun is 92,897,000 miles. The eccentricity of its orbit is $\frac{1}{60}$th, and the variation between its greatest and least distances about 3,000,000 miles. The figure of the earth, as already remarked, is that of an oblate spheroid—a sphere somewhat flattened at the poles and bulging out slightly at the equator. The spheroidal figure of the earth is due to the centrifugal force generated by its diurnal rotation on its axis. If we suppose the earth to have been originally in a fluid state, the effect of such a force would be to heap up the fluid material at the equator by drawing it away from the regions around the poles, and the figure which the earth would assume under such circumstances would continue to exist when the earth arrived at its present condition of a solid body partially covered by an aqueous fluid. In fact, it appears, from the lengths of the earth's diameters given below, that the waters of the ocean are piled up at the equator 13½ miles higher relatively to the earth's centre than they are at the poles ; and if it were not for the continual rotation of this mass of fluid round the earth's axis it would flow towards the poles, and alter completely the distribution of land and water at present existing.

The science of Geodesy is concerned with the accurate measurement of the size and figure of the earth. Its fundamental astronomical problem is to determine the length of a degree of latitude or longitude at various places on the surface of the globe. On such measures depends our knowledge of the shape or figure of the earth. It has been found that the length of a degree of latitude is not the same at all parts of the earth's surface, but increases slightly from the equator to the poles. This is the result of the flattening at the poles and the protuberance around the equatorial regions. From the various measures made at different parts of the earth it has been shown that the equatorial diameter is 7927 miles and the polar diameter 7900 miles. Different equatorial diameters are also shown to be of different lengths, but the amount of their variation is small, the diameter joining the point of the equator in 8° 15′ west longitude to the opposite point, 188° 15′ west, being some 1000 yards longer than the diameter at right angles to it. The earth is therefore not strictly a spheroid, but a figure to which the name gloid has been applied.

The density of the earth, or its weight compared with the weight of the same volume of water, has been determined by several methods. In 1774-76 experiments for this purpose were made by Maskelyne, then Astronomer-Royal, on the effect of the attraction of the mountain Schiehallion on plumb-lines set up to the north and south of it. The direction of a plumb-line produced would pass through the zenith, or point exactly overhead, if it were not affected by the attraction of a mass of material sufficient to draw it out of the vertical. Each of the plumb-lines set up by Maskelyne would be drawn towards the mountain, and the north one would point north of the zenith, the south one south of it. The amount of these deflections were measured by astronomical observations, and from them the proportion between the attraction of the earth and that of the mountain on the plumb was determined. The mountain was then carefully surveyed to obtain its volume, and the density of the materials of which it is composed was obtained by experiment. The result showed that the density of the earth was about five times that of water. Another method, invented by Cavendish, compared the attraction of the earth with that of a leaden ball of known size and density. The dimensions and density of such a ball could be more accurately determined than those of an irregular mountain mass, composed of a variety of materials; but, on the other hand, the attraction of the ball is much smaller, and therefore more difficult to measure, than that of the mountain. Sir George Airy made a series of experiments with pendulums in Harton coal pit for the same purpose. The result of all these observations gave a value for the density of the earth of 5·5 times that of water. In recent years other refined methods of determining this constant have been devised, and the various results agree remarkably with the value stated, considering the great delicacy of the measures involved.

The phenomena of the tides, illustrated in figs. 3 and 4 of Plate II., arise from the combined attraction which the sun and moon exercise on the water on the earth's surface. Each of these bodies exerts a separate influence on the water, and would of itself produce a tide independent of that produced by the other. Each tends to heap up the water of the oceans in its own direction, and also on the opposite side of the earth. The attraction of either body on the water on the side of the earth turned towards it is greater than its attraction on the solid mass of the earth itself, and this is again greater than the attraction exerted on the water on the opposite side. There is, therefore, a tendency to heap up the water immediately under the attracting body, while the earth is drawn away from the water on the opposite side, leaving it somewhat behind, and producing the effect of a rise of tide. The illustrations show clearly the rise of tide at opposite sides of the earth's surface.

The moon produces a greater effect by its attraction in the formation of the tides than the sun does, for, though the sun is of enormously greater mass than the moon, the latter is very much nearer to the earth. Its closeness to the earth more than compensates for its smaller mass. The lunar tide is about two and a half times as great as the solar. When sun and moon act along the same line, the resulting tides are equal to the sum of the tides produced by each of these bodies acting separately. This is the case both at new moon, when the latter is between the earth and sun, as well as at full moon, when the two bodies are at opposite sides of the earth. The tides so formed are called *spring* tides (fig. 4, Plate II.). On the other hand, when sun and moon act along lines at right angles to one another—that is, when the moon is at first and last quarter—the solar tide is subtracted from the lunar, and the resulting tide, called *neap* tide (fig. 3, Plate II.), is the difference of the two. In every other position of the sun and moon with respect to the earth the two bodies act partly against one another. In all cases the combined effect tends to cause the earth to assume the shape of an ellipsoid, the longer axis of which is directed to the principal tide-producing body, the moon. As the earth rotates on its axis from west to east the heaping up of the water moves towards the west, causing high tide twice a day at all places accessible to the water of the oceans. The moon arrives at the meridian of a place about 50 minutes later each day, hence each high tide is followed by another after 12 hours 25 minutes, and by a second after 24 hours 50 minutes on an average. Though, theoretically, the effect of attraction is to keep the longer axis of the tidal ellipsoid directed towards the moon, the conformation of the land surface of the globe produces a different practical result. High water does not occur when the moon is on the meridian of the place of observation, but after an interval which has to be determined for each place. At new and full moon the interval which elapses between noon and the time of high water is known as the *establishment of the port*. This interval is less at places open to the ocean and greater up the estuaries, by the shores of which the flow of the tide is restricted. Thus at the Scilly Islands the establishment of the port is about 4 hours 27 minutes, and at Bristol about 7 hours 13 minutes.

The planet MARS is distinguishable from the other bright planets by its red colour. Its mean distance from the sun is 141,550,000 miles, least distance

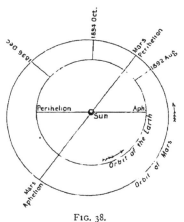

FIG. 38.

Oppositions of Mars.

128,300,000 miles, and greatest 154,700,000. The eccentricity of its orbit is about one-tenth, or nearly six times as great as that of the earth's orbit. The diameter of the planet is 4180 miles, or little more than half that of the earth, and its mass about one-ninth that of the earth, or about $\frac{1}{3000000}$th that of the sun. The disc exhibits a slight compression at the polar regions, amounting to $\frac{1}{190}$th of its diameter, which, though greater relatively than the compression of the earth's poles, is yet so small as to be very difficult of measurement. There are reasons for believing that Mars possesses an atmosphere much rarer than the earth's.

The synodical period of Mars is 780 days, or nearly 2 years 2 months. This is the time which elapses between two successive oppositions. It will be remembered that the outer planets are most easily observed when they are not far from this position, as they are then nearer the earth, than under other circumstances. The oppositions do not all take place under exactly similar conditions. Fig. 38 shows the position of the perihelion of Mars with respect to the earth's aphelion, and the points at which a few oppositions have taken place. It will be noticed that the two orbits lie closest to one another between perihelion of Mars and aphelion of the earth. When opposition takes place at this region of the sky, as in 1892, Mars comes closer to the earth than at other oppositions. These closest oppositions occur at intervals of seven synodical periods, or about fifteen years. Mars appears then much brighter than at oppositions occurring at the other side of the orbit, and the increased lustre fully justifies its name, the "fiery red planet." This is due to two reasons—because being then nearer to the sun the planet receives more light from it; and, again, the earth being close to Mars receives more reflected light. The distance between Mars and the earth at opposition varies from 35,000,000 miles in the most favourable conditions to 61,000,000 when Mars is at aphelion.

The orbit of Mars being outside that of the earth, this planet is never seen under the crescent form. The disc is usually round, except when near the position of quadrature—that is, when a line from the earth to Mars would be at right angles to one from the earth to the sun. It then assumes the gibbous form. When the unenlightened part of the disc is at its greatest it appears in shape like the moon two or three days from full.

The two satellites of Mars, Phobos and Deimos, were discovered by Professor Asaph Hall in 1877 with the great telescope of the Washington Observatory. They are both very small, probably not more than 6 or 7 miles in diameter, Phobos being somewhat the larger. Phobos revolves about its primary in 7 hours 39 minutes at 6000 miles distance, and Deimos in 30 hours 18 minutes at a distance of about 15,000 miles, both nearly in the equator of Mars. Mars rotates on its axis in 24 hours 37 minutes 23 seconds. Phobos, therefore, so far as is known, occupies the unique position in the solar system of a satellite revolving about its primary in less time than the primary takes to rotate on its axis. It follows that Phobos must rise in the west, to an observer on Mars, and set in the east. On the earth we are accustomed to think of a star or planet rising above the eastern horizon, because the earth's rotation carries the horizon down to and below it. To this rule our moon conforms. Phobos, so far from being overtaken by the eastern horizon of an observer on Mars, itself overtakes the western horizon from below, rises above it, and in due time sinks below the eastern. This its rapid angular motion enables it to do at least twice a day. Deimos, the outer of the two moons, has an angular movement in its orbit round Mars less than that of Mars on its axis, but so great that this satellite may remain above the horizon of a point on the planet for about two and a half days at a time.

Up to the middle of the nineteenth century little was known about the surface condition of Mars beyond the white patches around the Polar regions, which were early recognised as snows, from the fact that they were seen to increase in the winter season and decrease in the summer of their respective hemispheres. Some irregular dark patches had also been seen, and drawings made of them. It was also believed that the planet was surrounded by an atmosphere. Later on, the permanency of these dark markings was recognised, and they were looked upon as seas, the brighter portions of the surface being considered land. There were also reasons for supposing that the atmosphere was much more rarefied than ours, and less capable of being charged with cloud. The land surface is more extensive in proportion to sea than on the earth, the southern hemisphere being nearly covered with the dark patches, or so-called seas, the northern with the brighter areas, supposed to be land.

Within the past few years the researches of many eminent astronomers have resulted in a great extension of our knowledge of this planet. We have space to refer only to those of Schiaparelli at Milan, and of Mr Percival Lowell at Flagstaff, Arizona. It must be remembered that the details of planetary markings are amongst the most difficult of astronomical observations. The finer details require not only adequate telescopic aid, but also the most perfect atmospheric conditions. Schiaparelli studied the planet at the 1877 and following oppositions, and mapped a network of dark lines crossing the bright, or continental, regions from sea to sea. To those lines he gave the name of canals. They cross one another, some at right angles, others obliquely, and all terminate either in one of the seas or in other canals. Schiaparelli's most remarkable discovery as to the surface of Mars was that the canals appeared to become double at certain seasons. This took place all over the continental portions of the planet. Mr Percival Lowell's observations were made at Flagstaff, Arizona, where, owing to the wonderful steadiness of the atmosphere, he had unusual opportunities for the pursuit of such work. His study of the planet at the opposition of 1894-95 has led him to the conclusion that the canals are artificially constructed by an intelligent race of inhabitants for the purpose of irrigation. There appears to be no reason to suppose that Mars is not inhabited. The amount of water is comparatively small. What is more reasonable than to suppose that the inhabitants should try to rectify the deficiency by a system of canals, which the flatness of the continental surface renders easy of accomplishment. What has been seen by the fortunate observers, who have the proper instrumental and atmospheric conditions at their disposal, are not the canals themselves, but the growth of vegetation along their borders. The impossibility of accounting for the existing markings from natural causes appears "upon three distinct counts, first the straightness of the lines ; second, their individually uniform width ; third, their systematic radiation from different points." In his third count Mr Lowell refers to the meeting of three or more canals at a large number of points on the surface. It seems impossible that such numerous convergences could be accidental. Seasonal changes which were noticed in the dark regions, hitherto called seas, of the southern hemisphere are explained by supposing that the blue-green colour of this part of the planet's surface is due to vegetation, and that there are no large bodies of water of a permanent character on the planet.

The ASTEROIDS, or minor planets, have already been referred to on p. 37. In the early days of their discovery Olbers suggested that they were the fragments of a planet which once occupied the space between Mars and Jupiter. In 1891 Max Wolf of Heidelberg commenced to search for asteroids by photography. He has been successful in adding over sixty to the list. Charlois, of the Nice Observatory, has discovered nearly 100 by the same method.

JUPITER is the largest of all the planets. Its equatorial diameter is 88,700 miles, or more than eleven times that of the earth. Its polar diameter is 82,800 miles, and the globe is compressed to the extent of $\frac{1}{15}$th of the equatorial diameter. Its volume is 1312 times that of the earth ; but its mass, or the quantity of matter contained within its boundaries, is only 318 times that of the earth. It follows that the density of Jupiter is less than a quarter of the earth's. The planet rotates on its axis in 9 hours 55 minutes, and revolves about the sun in 11·86 years, at a mean distance of 483,288,000 miles.

There are many reasons for believing that Jupiter is surrounded by an atmosphere of great extent. The ceaseless changes in the aspect of its surface, the general parallelism of the belts to the equator, and the situation of the most prominent of them near the equatorial regions, support this opinion. The spectrum of the light reflected from its surface also shows certain dark shadings, which are supposed to be due to absorption by the planet's atmosphere of a part of this light.

Viewed in the telescope, the surface of Jupiter is seen to be marked by dusky greyish streaks, called belts, which vary in number and breadth, and are usually parallel to the planet's equator. They are to be explained as openings in the cloudy atmosphere, through which the lower lying strata are visible. Sometimes spots are seen on the surface. The most interesting of these in recent times was the "great red spot" which appeared in 1878, and remained visible till 1883 or 1884, when it faded for a time, but afterwards reappeared, and continued to be a remarkable telescopic object for many years. In 1880 an oval white spot appeared. Attempts were made to determine the rotation period by observation of these spots. It was found, however, that they had a motion with reference to the body of the planet, so that no reliance could be placed on the period found from them. The period given above — 9 hours 55 minutes—was determined by Sir G. Airy in 1835.

Jupiter is accompanied in its orbit round the sun by seven satellites. Four of these were discovered by Galileo in 1610, and may be seen with very slight telescopic assistance. The fifth was discovered by Barnard at the Lick Observatory in California in 1892; the sixth and seventh by Prof. Perrine at the same Observatory in December 1904 and February 1905. The four earlier discovered are named Io, Europa, Ganymede, Callisto. They are more usually known, however, as the 1st, 2nd, 3rd, and 4th satellites, in the order of their distances from the planet, the 4th being the farthest. The fifth is nearer to the planet than the four older ones; the sixth and seventh are the outer members of the group.

The following table gives the distances of the satellites from their primary, and other particulars :—

| | Discoverer and Date. | Mean Distance from Centre of Planet. | | Time of Sidereal Revolution. | | | Diameter in Miles. |
		Radius of Planet I.	Miles.	D.	H.	M.	
V.	Barnard, 1892 .	2·55	111,800	0	11	57	...
I.	Galileo, 1610 .	5·93	260,000	1	18	28	2349
II.	,, ,,	9·44	413,900	3	13	14	2107
III.	,, ,,	15·06	660,400	7	3	43	3442
IV.	,, ,,	26·49	1,162,000	16	16	32	2945
VI.	Prof. Perrine, 1904 .	72·80	3,192,000	251	0	0	...
VII.	,, ,, 1905 .	94·93	4,162,700	265	0	0	...

The revolutions of the satellites about their primary present an interesting series of phenomena as seen from the earth. Eclipses of the 1st, 2nd, and 3rd satellites take place at every revolution round Jupiter. Eclipses of the 4th occur more rarely, its orbit being more inclined to the ecliptic. Occultations occur when the satellites are hidden from view behind the body of the planet. Transits are the passages of the satellites across the disc of the planet, when they appear as white spots on the surface, and are usually preceded or followed by their shadows, which appear as black spots.

The eclipses of Jupiter's satellites being visible at the same instant of time at every point of the earth's surface turned towards the planet at the moment, it was perceived at an early date that observations of them would be available for determining the difference of local time at two places, or, in other words, the difference of longitude. If once accurate predictions of the times of the eclipses could be made from a complete knowledge of a satellite's movements, these predictions would give the local time at the observatory for which they were calculated. An observation of the transit at any place for which local time was known accurately would then give the required difference of longitude. This method of finding longitudes may be said to have been practically super-seded in favour of others. It led Römer, however, in 1675 to a very remarkable discovery—that of the gradual propagation of light through space. Römer, in the course of his investigation of one of the satellites, observed a large number of its eclipses, and found that the observed times of eclipse did not always agree with the predicted times. On examining this apparent anomaly with care, he found that the observed time of an eclipse was always later than the predicted when the earth was far away from Jupiter, and earlier when the earth was close to Jupiter. These phenomena presented themselves with such regularity that it became evident to Römer they must in some way depend on the distance of the earth from Jupiter. As an explanation he suggested the gradual propagation of light through space, and, on this supposition, calculated that light takes sixteen and a half minutes to cross the diameter of the earth's orbit. Römer's discovery awaited confirmation for many years, no other pheno-menon being known to show an effect which could be explained in the same way. The confirmation came when Bradley, in the middle of the eighteenth century, made the remarkable discovery of the aberration of light. The only explanation of this latter phenomenon is that light travels at a rate which is comparable with, though enormously greater than, the rate at which the earth moves in its orbit. Laboratory experiments by many physicists have since shown that the speed of light is 180,000 miles per second. It therefore takes 8 minutes 17 seconds to traverse the mean distance between the earth and sun.

The small density of Jupiter indicates that it is, to a larger extent than any of the planets to which we have as yet referred, composed of gases and vapours surrounding a small amount of solid matter. Such a condition existing in such an enormous mass, where the force of gravity is excessive, can only be explained by supposing the interior to be at a high temperature, the visible surface being an envelope of cloud composed of gases condensed by radiation of heat into space. Unlike the earth and Mars, Jupiter has not yet cooled down sufficiently to be a fit residence for human beings.

SATURN is the second largest of all the planets. Its diameter is 75,100 miles, or about nine and a third times the diameter of the earth. Its volume is 763 times that of the earth, but its mass is only ninety-five times the earth's. Its mean density is therefore only one-eighth of the earth's, or about seven-tenths of the density of water. It revolves on its axis in 10 hours 14 minutes. As the result of this rapid rotation, combined with its small density—less than that of the sun or any other of the planets—a considerable protuberance about the equatorial regions and flattening of the poles might be anticipated. Measurement has shown that these exist, the polar diameter having been found less than the equatorial by 7900 miles.

At the time of opposition Saturn appears to the naked eye as bright as a star of the first magnitude. In the telescope its surface is found to be diversified by a number of faint belts extending across the disc in a direction parallel to the equator, and lying chiefly in the equatorial regions. In this and some other respects Saturn resembles Jupiter. Its very small density points to the existence of a high temperature in the interior of the planet. Saturn, like Jupiter, probably consists mainly of gases and vapours with but little solid matter, and is encompassed by an extensive cloudy atmosphere which prevents us from seeing the real surface of the planet.

Saturn is attended by ten satellites. The following table gives their names, dates of discovery, and other particulars :—

Name and Order of Distance from Primary.	Name of Discoverer and Date.	Mean Distance from Centre of Planet.		Time of Revolution.		
		Radius of Planet = 1.	Miles.	D.	H.	M.
1. Mimas	Sir Wm. Herschel, 1789	3·07	116,050	0	22	37
2. Enceladus.	,, ,, ,,	3·94	148,930	1	8	53
3. Tethys	J. D. Cassini, 1684	4·87	184,100	1	21	18
4. Dione	,, ,, ,,	6·25	236,250	2	17	41
5. Rhea	,, ,, 1672	8·73	330,000	4	12	25
6. Titan	Huyghens, 1655	20·22	764,300	15	22	41
10. Themis	W. H. Pickering, 1905	24·14	912,500	20	20	24
7. Hyperion	Bond and Lassell, 1848.	24·49	925,700	21	6	38
8. Iapetus	J. D. Cassini, 1671	58·91	2,227,000	79	7	56
9. Phœbe	W. H. Pickering, 1898	214·4	8,090,700	500	10	34

The ninth satellite was discovered by Professor W. H. Pickering, of Lowell Observatory, Flagstaff, Arizona, an observatory already notable for the investigation of the surfaces of Mars and other planets made there. The discovery was made by photography, traces of the satellite being found on four plates, each exposed for about two hours on the nights of 16th, 17th, and 18th August 1898. The satellite is of about the fifteenth magnitude, and therefore too faint to be seen in any but large instruments. The tenth was the discovery of the same astronomer in 1905. As will be seen from the table, its mean distance from the primary is between those of Titan and Hyperion, but its orbit overlaps that of both the neighbouring satellites.

All the satellites revolve round their primary nearly in the plane of the ring, which coincides with the plane of the equator, except Iapetus, Phœbe, and Themis, whose orbits are inclined to the equator at angles of about 10^c, 147°, and 11° respectively. Titan is by far the largest of the satellites, and was the first discovered. Its diameter is over 3000 miles, or about three-quarters of the diameter of Mars. It is the only one of the satellites of Saturn that can be seen with moderate telescopic assistance. The innermost satellites more especially can only be seen with telescopes of superior power and in the most favourable atmospheric conditions.

Saturn is unique amongst the planets of the solar system in the possession of a system of broad flat rings surrounding it and separated from it on all sides. The rings lie all in the same plane, which is inclined to the ecliptic at an angle of 28° 6'. As we can look at Saturn only from the point we occupy in the ecliptic, it follows that the rings can never be seen with their full face turned towards us. If we could see them in a direction perpendicular to their plane they would appear circular in form. As it is, we can only see them either obliquely or edge on. They, therefore, present to our eyes the foreshortened appearance of ellipses more or less elongated, or of a straight line in the extreme case when their edge is turned towards us. The plane of the rings cuts the ecliptic in two points, called the *nodes*. When the planet reaches a certain point in its orbit round the sun, the line joining the centre of the planet to one of the nodes of the ring produced will pass through the sun. In this position the edge only of the rings is illuminated, and we see it as a very thin line stretching out radially from the body of the planet on both sides. Sometimes the rings disappear from view altogether. This happens when the line joining Saturn's centre to a node of the ring passes between the earth and the sun. The illuminated side of the rings is then turned away from the earth, and the side presented to the earth is dark. As Saturn advances in its orbit the ring plane will appear to open out. At first a very elongated ellipse, the breadth gradually increases till one-quarter of the orbit has been passed from the point of disappearance. Here the ellipse is of its greatest apparent breadth, and the minor axis has now become nearly equal to half the major axis. From this point the opening decreases till another quarter of the orbit has been completed, when the rings again become a straight line, and disappear. In the remaining half of the orbit similar phases recur, but now the opposite surface of the rings is visible from the earth. A disappearance of the rings took place on 22nd September 1891, and they remained invisible up to 30th October of that year. From this date the north surface of the rings was turned towards the earth, and remained visible up to April 1907. From April to July the rings were invisible, their plane passing between the earth and sun. After this the south surface was visible up to October, when they again disappeared. After January 1908 the south surface remained visible till 1921, when the rings again disappeared, and later reappeared, the north surface being now visible. The phases of the rings are illustrated in Plate I. A view of the planet, from a drawing by Mr De La Rue, will be found in Plate VIII. The shadows cast by the ring on the body of the planet, and by the planet on the part of the ring opposite the sun, are well shown. These shadows are sufficient proof that both rings and planet are opaque, and shine by the reflected light of the sun.

Galileo first detected the existence of some sort of appendage to the planet. Its real nature was first discovered by the Dutch astronomer Huyghens in the middle of the seventeenth century. In 1676 J. D. Cassini discovered that the supposed single ring really consisted of two rings, separated by a narrow black streak. A third and much fainter ring was discovered in 1850 by Bond, an American astronomer, and almost simultaneously by Dawes in England. It lies inside the other two, and is known as the *dark* ring, and can be seen only in large telescopes. It is considered certain that the rings consist of numberless small bodies, each revolving as a satellite about the planet. The whole ring system has a motion of rotation round the body of the planet in 10 hours 32 minutes, and it has recently been determined by actual measurement that the body of the planet is not placed quite centrally within the rings. To these two facts it has been shown that the stability of the ring system is due.

URANUS comes next to Saturn in the order of distance from the sun. Its diameter is 31,000 miles, and a polar compression of one-thirteenth or one-fourteenth has been measured by some observers. On account of its great distance its apparent diameter varies but little, and, when at its greatest, is less than 4″. It is attended by four satellites, particulars of which will be found in the following table:—

Name.	Discoverer and Date.	Mean Distance.		Sidereal Revolution.		
		Radius of Planet=1.	Miles.	D.	H.	M.
1. Ariel .	Lassell, Oct. 24, 1851 . .	7·04	118,300	2	12	29
2. Umbriel .	,, ,, ,, . .	9·91	166,500	4	3	28
3. Titania .	Sir W. Herschel, Jan. 11, 1787	16·11	270,600	8	16	56
4. Oberon .	,, ,, ,, ,,	21·54	361,900	13	11	7

The orbits of the satellites of Uranus are inclined to the ecliptic at an angle of 82°, and the motion of the satellites is retrograde, or contrary to the order of the signs of the Zodiac.

Uranus was discovered by Sir Wm. Herschel in 1781. He was engaged examining the stars in a portion of the constellation Gemini when he noticed one which struck him as peculiar in appearance. Measurements of its position showed him that it moved amongst the stars, and must therefore be either a comet or a planet. The computation of its orbit showed that it was a planet

G

revolving round the sun in an ellipse of very small eccentricity. Its period of revolution is eighty-four years, and its distance from the sun varies from 1,699,000,000 miles to 1,866,000,000, the mean distance being 1,782,800,000.

Owing to its great distance and small apparent diameter little or nothing is known of the physical appearance of the planet. Equatorial belts similar to those of Saturn and Jupiter have been suspected by one or two observers, but the disc is generally described as uniformly bluish in colour, without visible markings of any kind. The period of its rotation is between ten and eleven hours.

NEPTUNE is, so far as is at present known, the outermost planet of the solar system. It was discovered in 1846 by means of theoretical computations made by Mr Adams, in England, and M. Le Verrier, in France, on the perturbations which it produces on the movements of its nearest neighbour Uranus. It was first actually seen by Dr Galle of Berlin on 23rd September 1846, as the result of a successful systematic search in the place pointed out by Le Verrier. The priority of discovery by computation is therefore claimed for the French astronomer, though Adams certainly appears to have been the first to complete the computation necessary for determining the place of the planet. The possibility of the existence of a planet revolving about the sun in an orbit outside that of Neptune has been suggested.

Neptune revolves round the sun in 165 years, at a distance varying from 2,769,000,000 miles to 2,818,000,000, the mean distance being 2,793,500,000 miles. Its diameter is 33,000 miles. It has one satellite, the motion of which in its orbit is, like that of the satellites of Uranus, retrograde. The revolution of the satellite about its primary occupies 5 days 21 hours 3 minutes, at a distance from it of 222,000 miles.

CHAPTER XIII.

COMETS AND METEORS.

COMETS consist generally of a hazy, luminous head, accompanied by a long train of light, known as the tail. The head usually contains, at or near its centre, a bright star-like point called the nucleus, the most condensed part of the comet's substance. Round this appears the coma, shading out from the nucleus and forming with it the head. The tail, the least substantial part, emanates from the coma and stretches out into space, in a direction opposite to that of the sun. Many of the smaller telescopic comets, and even some of the brighter, show no trace of a tail during the whole time of their visibility. As a rule, however, when first seen in the telescope, in an early stage of their journey towards the sun, comets appear as a faint nebula, increasing in brightness night after night. As they approach nearer the sun the tail makes its appearance. The interesting fact that the tail is usually directed away from the sun was known to astronomers as early as the sixteenth century. It has since been established as a general law affecting all comets. The theory of the structure and growth of the tail has long been a subject of intense interest to astronomers, and many suggestions have been put forward in explanation. One theory which receives much support is that the comet and the sun are charged with electricity of similar kind. From this arises a repulsive force, which is capable of overpowering the force of gravitation, so far as the most attenuated parts of the comet's substance are concerned, while the denser portions are, of course, actuated by the force of the sun's attraction. Another, and perhaps more generally accepted theory is that the repulsive force is due to the pressure of light arising from the action of the sun's rays. In each of these theories the energy of the force of attraction depends on the masses of the bodies concerned, whereas that of the repulsive force depends on their surfaces. The mass, and hence the attractive force, decreases in proportion to the cubes of the diameter, while the surfaces decrease only as the squares of the diameter. Hence a point of minuteness is reached at which the lighter particles are more influenced by repulsion than by attraction. The main body of the comet is thus kept moving in its orbit about the sun, while the lighter particles are driven away from the sun to form the tail.

Professor Bredichin, Director of the Moscow Observatory, after an elaborate investigation into the repulsive force exerted by the sun's electrical condition on comets, resulting in the formation of the tails, came to the conclusion that these appendages were of three distinct types, and that each type was formed by a repellent energy bearing a certain fixed proportion to the attractive energy. In the first type the tail is long and comparatively straight, like those of the great comets of 1843 and 1882. This type of tail is probably formed of hydrogen, the lightest known substance, and therefore the most easily affected by the repulsive forces. In the second type the tails are curved to some extent, and are of more moderate length, like that of Donati's comet. In this type the hydrocarbons are supposed to be the principal components. In the third type the tails are comparatively short, still more curved than those of the second type, and brush-like in appearance. These tails are probably composed of particles of iron and other metals, and are usually found in combination with others of the first or second type, some of the brighter comets having two, or even three, tails. Some other substances are also known to be present in the composition of comets—sodium, magnesium, and nitrogen, as well as hydrogen and iron, having been detected in the great comet of 1882. The spectroscope has shown that there is no material difference between the spectra of the various parts of a comet.

The ancient philosophers believed that comets existed in the earth's atmosphere. This idea was first exploded by Tycho Brahe, who showed by actual measurements that the comet of 1577 moved in space at a distance from the earth farther away than the moon, and therefore far beyond the confines of the earth's atmosphere. Newton proved that the movements of comets, like those of the planets, are governed by the attraction of the sun ; and he further demonstrated that the great comet of 1680 moved in an orbit which was practically a parabola with the sun at the focus. The parabola, like the ellipse, is a conic section, but differs from the latter in that it is not a closed curve, but consists of two branches extending away into infinite space. A comet moving in such an orbit would approach the solar system along one branch, pass round the sun, and pursuing its course along the other branch, would disappear into space never to visit our sun again. A very eccentric or greatly elongated ellipse differs so little from a parabola, when account is taken only of that portion of it near the focus, that an orbit may be computed from observations, necessarily made when the comet is comparatively near the sun, on the supposition that it moves in a parabola. The elements of such a parabolic orbit would be sufficient for the purpose of predicting the movements of the comet for a considerable time, but the period of revolution could not be computed, as the curve is not a closed one. Newton therefore suggested that the elements of the orbits of all comets of which there existed sufficiently trustworthy observations should be computed and compared with one another, in order to find whether any two or more had elements so exactly alike as to amount to the certainty that they were apparitions of the same comet. The intervals between the apparitions would be an indication of the time of revolution. The celebrated Edmund Halley, Astronomer-Royal from 1720 to 1742, undertook the investigation of this problem. He determined the parabolic elements of the orbits of twenty-four comets, and on examination found that those of the remarkable comet of 1862 agreed so closely with those of the comets of 1607 and 1531 that he had no hesitation in declaring that they were three apparitions of the same comet, moving in an elliptic orbit with a periodic time of about seventy-five or seventy-six years. He predicted that the comet would return in the end of 1758 or beginning of 1759. The fulfilment of this, the first prediction of the return of a comet, was awaited, as the date approached, with great interest, and

Halley's prediction was justified by the appearance of the expected comet, which was announced in December 1758. The perihelion passage took place on 12th March 1759. The comet has been named after the renowned discoverer of its periodic character. Its distance from the sun was found to be 54,000,000 miles at perihelion, and 3,258,000,000 at aphelion. Hence at perihelion the comet was well inside the orbit of the earth, and at aphelion 500,000,000 miles beyond the orbit of Neptune. Halley's comet appeared again in 1835, the perihelion passage occurring on the 16th of November of that year. At its next appearance it was found on photographic plates exposed at Heidelberg on 11th September 1909, and at Greenwich on plates exposed on 9th September 1909. Pictures of it were obtained by photography at the Yerkes Observatory in April and May of 1910. This was the first comet known to be periodic. There are now about thirty known to revolve about the sun in elliptic orbits with periods of less than 100 years. Of these, however, only eighteen have been actually seen at two or more apparitions. The following table gives a list of these, with their periodic times, perihelion and aphelion distances, and number of recorded apparitions, the distances being referred to the earth's mean distance from the sun as the unit of measure :—

Name.	Sidereal Revolution in Years.	Distance.		Number of Apparitions observed.
		Perihelion.	Aphelion.	
1. Encke	3·30	0·34	4·10	29
2. Tempel . . .	5·28	1·39	4·68	5
3. Brorsen . . .	5·46	0·59	5·61	5
4. Tempel-Switt . .	5·68	1·15	5·21	3
5. Winnecke . .	5·83	0·92	5·55	7
6. De Vico . .	6·40	1·67	5·22	3
7. Tempel . . .	6·54	2·09	4·90	3
8. Finlay . . .	6·54	0·97	6·03	3
9. D'Arrest . .	6·69	1·32	6·77	6
10. Biela . . .	6·69	0·88	6·22	6
11. Wolf . . .	6·82	1·60	5·60	3
12. Holmes . . .	6·86	2·12	5·10	3
13. Brooks . . .	7·10	1·96	5·43	3
14. Faye . . .	7·39	1·65	5·94	8
15. Tuttle . . .	13·67	1·02	10·41	5
16. Pons-Brooks . .	71·56	0·78	33·70	2
17. Olbers . . .	72·65	1·20	33·62	2
18. Halley . . .	76·08	0·69	35·22	23

It will be noticed that of these comets Encke's has the shortest period, and also comes closest to the sun at perihelion. No. 10 of the list, Biela's comet, at its apparition in 1846 divided into two parts, both of which appeared again in 1852, separated from one another by more than 1,000,000 miles. Nothing has since been seen of either part with certainty, though an observation made of a comet in 1872 by the late Mr Pogson of Madras may have been Biela's. There are several other known instances of comets breaking up into two or more fragments. As we will see later, there is no doubt an intimate connection between comets and meteors, and it is possible that the disintegration of the former bodies is the source of at least some of the meteoric showers. Thus the shower known as the Andromedes, seen in the end of November, is thought to be composed of fragments of the lost Biela comet, remarkably brilliant displays of these meteors having occurred in 1872, 1885, and in 1892.

No. 13 of the above list, Brooks' comet, at its first known apparition was accompanied by four fragments, seen as feeble telescopic objects. A large number of known apparitions is credited to Halley's comet. These include, however, many apparitions in past centuries which have been identified with Halley's, after the orbits had been computed from the best authentic records of observations. The earliest dates from 12 B.C.

Besides the comets with periods less than 100 years, about as many more are known to revolve round the sun in very elongated ellipses, having periods amounting in some cases to hundreds of years, in other cases to thousands. None of these have as yet been identified on their return to perihelion.

It is an interesting fact that a number of the periodic comets may be arranged in groups, each group having the aphelion positions of the several comets belonging to it close to the orbit of one of the four great planets. There are eighteen whose orbits reach out close to the orbit of Jupiter, two similarly belong to Saturn, three to Uranus, and six to Neptune. It is supposed that they may have originally moved in parabolic orbits, but coming at one time or other close to a planet of large mass, they were drawn by its attraction out of their original orbits, and forced to move henceforth in ellipses. The mass of Jupiter being so much greater than that of any of the other planets, it has been successful in capturing the largest number of comets.

It has been mentioned that the identity of two apparitions of the same comet is established by the similarity of the elements of their orbits computed from observation of their movements. Their appearance, either in the telescope or to the naked eye, affords no clue to their identity, because they vary much both in form and brightness from one apparition to another. Sometimes even the similarity of orbits is not sufficient to prove that the appearances in separate years are in reality of one and the same object. This is most strikingly exemplified in the case of the great comet of 1882. This remarkable comet was first seen early in September of that year. It was then approaching the sun, and its progress was followed by many observers. At the Cape of Good Hope Observatory it was seen to come right up to the sun's edge, where it disappeared from view, passing across the sun's disc, and reappearing the following day, 18th September. It was then seen to be a magnificent object. As soon as its orbit was computed it was found to bear a very close resemblance to those of the comets of 1843 and 1880. One remarkable fact was the length of time this comet remained visible, being still a naked-eye object up to March 1883, and up to May or June it was still to be seen as a faint object in the telescope. There was thus ample opportunity of determining its orbit with the greatest certainty. It proved to be moving in a very eccentric elliptic orbit, with a period of several hundreds of years. The length of the period at once disposes of the possibility of identifying it with its predecessors of 1843 and 1880, in spite of the similarity of orbits. This similarity, however, combined with the long period, gives the clue to the true explanation of the relationship between them, which is, that they are distinct bodies, following one another along the same orbit at irregular intervals, and it is allowable to surmise that there may be others also moving in the same track. In fact, the comet of 1887 has been shown to be a member of the same group. Some strange physical connection must exist between these bodies, probably indicating a common origin. The comet of 1882 was also remarkable for the curious appendage which appeared to envelope the coma and stretch out in the direction of the sun for a great distance. At perihelion the comet passed very close to the sun, the comparatively short distance of 300,000 miles alone separating it from the solar surface. This fact no doubt explains the splendour of the comet's appearance after perihelion passage, and the disintegration of the nucleus, which was seen to be divided into at least four portions.

It will be interesting to notice briefly a few other comets which were remarkable either for their splendour or for the addition to scientific knowledge which has followed the observation of them.

The comet of 1680 furnished to Newton the materials which enabled him to demonstrate that comets move in their orbits under the attractive influence of the sun. It is also remarkable for having approached within 120,000 miles of the sun's surface, or nearer than any other known comet, with the exception of that of 1843.

In 1811 there appeared one of the most splendid comets recorded in history. After perihelion passage, which took place in September, its tail presented a grand appearance, stretching over 25° of the sky, and measuring in absolute length about 100,000,000 miles.

Encke's comet was discovered at Marseilles by Pons in 1818. Encke found that it revolved in an elliptic orbit with a period of three and a half years, and that it had already appeared in 1786, 1795, and 1805. Many apparitions of it have since been observed. A curious circumstance connected with the periodic time of this comet was discovered. This was, that at each successive appearance the period of revolution was found to be somewhat shorter than the preceding. After every allowance had been made for planetary disturbances, Encke computed the time of revolution in 1819 to be precisely 1211·78 days ; in 1822 it had shortened to 1211·66 days ; and at the next apparition in 1825 it was only 1211·55 days. The same amount of shortening of the period went on up to 1858, when the period had fallen to 1210·44 days. This startling anomaly was accounted for by Encke on the theory that the comet's motion was retarded by a "resisting medium" pervading all space, and of extreme tenuity, though increasing in density towards the sun. Such a retardation, or slowing of the comet's motion, would result in its orbit becoming gradually smaller, and its period consequently would become shorter. A certain confirmation was given to this theory in 1880, when it was found that Winnecke's comet showed traces of a similar retardation of its motion, and the consequent shortening of its period. In later years, however, two circumstances appear to have thrown very considerable doubt on Encke's theory. In 1882 it was shown by Backlund, of the St. Petersburg Observatory, that the amount of the shortening of the period of the comet had suddenly altered in 1868. Whereas, previous to this date, the successive apparitions occurred at intervals each one-tenth of a day, or over two hours shorter than the last, after 1868 they were only shortened by less than three-fourths of that amount. This could not be accounted for on the theory of a resisting medium. The observations of the comet of 1882 threw still further doubt on Encke's theory. This comet, as we have already seen, passed within less than 300,000 miles of the sun's surface. So close an approach to the sun must necessarily have subjected its motion to a much greater retardation than that of Encke's from the resisting medium, if such existed. This comet was carefully observed, and its rate of motion obtained for a week at least before its perihelion passage, and for several months after it, but no trace of retardation could be found. The anomalous motion of Encke's comet, therefore, still awaits explanation.

The great comet of 1843 is remarkable as having been seen in broad daylight in the immediate neighbourhood of the sun. It approached the sun to within a distance of 49,000 miles, or closer than any other comet known to history. Its enormous tail, stretching over a great part of the sky, measured 150,000,000 miles in length.

Donati's comet of 1858 was one of the grandest of the past century. It was first seen by Donati at the Florence Observatory on the 2nd June as a telescopic comet. It became visible to the naked eye in August, and its greatest splendour was reached in September and October. The absolute length of its tail was about 40,000,000 miles. On 5th October the bright star Arcturus could be seen shining through the densest part of the tail without any apparent enfeebling of its brilliancy. In September two secondary tails made their appearance; they were long and very thin rays, one being a tangent to the outer curve of the principal tail, the other was nearly parallel to it, and appeared to emanate from the opposite side of the comet's head. In 1881 a bright comet appeared of a type somewhat similar to Donati's. It was best seen in the northern hemisphere in June.

It has been already stated that the star Arcturus was seen shining with unimpaired brilliancy through nearly the densest part of Donati's comet of 1858. To this we may add that even very small stars have in many instances been seen shining through the coma or nebulosity surrounding the heads of comets. It might be inferred from this that the substance of which comets are composed is of extreme tenuity, and that their masses are quite inconsiderable. Observation has shown this to be the case. No trace of disturbance of the movements of any planet of the solar system has ever been produced by the close approach of a comet. Indeed, Lexell's comet, both in 1767 and in 1779, came so close to Jupiter that it must have passed between him and some of his satellites, without, however, producing the least derangement in the motion of the moons.

The great comet of 1847 was so bright that the round distinctly marked nucleus and some of the most luminous parts of the coma were visible at noonday. Drawings made of the comet of 1861 show that its head presented a most remarkable appearance as it approached the sun. Streams of luminous matter appeared to issue from the nucleus, and curve backward in the direction of the tail. Several photographic pictures of Comet Swift, 1892, were made by Professor Barnard at Yerkes Observatory. One of these, taken on the 4th of April, showed a large cloudy mass of the matter composing the tail separated out, and apparently drifting away from the head. The separation of this mass, which must have been expelled from the head by the repellent action of the sun, may have been due to the supply of the matter drawn from the nucleus being suddenly stopped, to break out again after a short interval. A photograph of Comet Brooks, 1893, also made by Professor Barnard on the night of 21st October, showed a well-marked head, round on the side nearest the sun, and a continuous but irregularly shaped tail. "On the preceding night," Professor Barnard says, "the comet had a gradually widening tail, with a second smaller tail making an angle of 20˚ or 30 with the principal one. On the night of the 22nd the tail was broken and hung in cloudy masses—an extraordinary object." Professor Barnard considers that this condition of the tail suggests the probability of its being due to its having encountered a resisting medium of some kind. Comet 1903, C, though visible to the naked eye for some time, was not a very conspicuous object. Photographs of it show that the tail was of very considerable length, and close to the head was made up of several distinct rays. The comet, like those of 1892 and 1893, showed the remarkable phenomenon of part of the tail breaking off and drifting away from the head.

The origin of the light by which comets are seen is not quite certain. On their near approach to the sun the great increase of light which they then exhibit almost certainly arises from the solar electrification, to which is also due the evolution of the tail. Some part of the light is also, without doubt, the reflected light of the sun.

The characteristic spectrum of comets consists of three bright bands, with a continuous spectrum of relatively feeble intensity. The bright bands, which are in the yellow, green, and blue parts of the spectrum, are sharply defined on the side nearest to the red, and shaded off on the side towards the violet. They coincide with three of the bands found in the spectra of the hydro-carbon gases. Spectroscopes of great dispersive power show them as series of rays forming more or less regular groups. In ordinary instruments the sharp edge is seen, with a slight shading off towards the violet. In some very bright comets the continuous spectrum was sufficiently strong to allow some of the dark Fraunhofer lines of the solar spectrum to be seen, showing that at least a small part of the light of comets is light reflected from the sun. In the comet of 1882 the sodium line was discovered by Dr Ralph Copeland in the spectrum of the nucleus and surrounding coma. The brightness of this line increased greatly in intensity as the comet approached perihelion, while, at the same time, the hydrocarbon bands became very faint. This fact has been interpreted as showing that the chief part of the light is due to electrical action, laboratory investigations having proved that only under electrical illumination do the spectra of these substances increase and decrease in brilliancy in this manner. Dr Copeland was also the first to observe in the spectrum of the same comet a number of bright lines in the yellow and green, which he identified as coinciding with some of the stronger lines in the spectrum of iron.

Comets which become visible at their approach to the sun probably form but a small proportion of the number actually existing in space. Telescopic comets have of late years been seen, on an average, about four or five in a year.

METEORS may be conveniently divided into three classes — Aerolites, Fireballs, and Shooting Stars. The researches of modern scientists have shown that these bodies are of cosmical origin, that is, they originate outside the bounds of the earth's atmosphere, and are, therefore, legitimately within the domain of astronomical science. There is no doubt but that the three classes are of like origin, differing principally in size and in the form in which they manifest themselves to our sight, and perhaps to some extent in chemical composition.

Aerolites are bodies of comparatively large size. They are known as Siderites when they are composed mainly of meteoric iron ; Siderolites when they consist of iron and stone, each in large proportions, the name Aerolite being more properly restricted to those which consist almost entirely of stone. Numerous instances might be cited of the fall of these bodies to the earth. Passing over several known or suspected cases in the records of ancient history, a few occurrences of this kind may be noted which are known within the past half century. On the 1st of May 1860 Guernsey County, Ohio, was the scene of a remarkable fall of meteoric stones. The event was proceded by loud explosions, and two of the stones were seen to descend with great velocity, and to bury themselves in the earth. More than thirty pieces were collected in a space 10 miles long by 3 broad, the largest of them weighing 103 lbs.

On 9th June 1866 an aerolite fell at Knyahina in Hungary which weighed upwards of 600 lbs. The fall was preceded by the appearance of a luminous globe, followed by an explosion accompanied by smoke. Besides the principal aerolite, about 1000 smaller stones fell.

A fine specimen of a siderite, now in the British Museum, fell in 1865 in Arabia. It weighs about 130 lbs.

On 25th June 1890 in Kansas, U.S.A., several observers saw a meteorite fall, leaving a trail of smoke, and bursting with a loud explosion. The principal portion, weighing 180 lbs., buried itself 4 feet deep in the earth. On being dug out it proved to be a fine aerolite.

The museums of London, Paris, Vienna, and Washington contain large collections of meteorites found in various parts of the world.

Meteoric iron is an alloy of iron with about 10 per cent. of nickel and traces of cobalt, copper, tin, carbon, manganese, and magnesium. A similar alloy of iron is not found amongst terrestrial minerals. Meteoric stone is somewhat similar in chemical composition to terrestrial mineral of volcanic origin, such as the trap rocks and lavas. No element has been found in meteorites which is not also known to exist on the earth.

Fireballs, or detonating meteors, probably differ little from aerolites. They appear as luminous globes, which are seen to traverse the atmosphere with great velocity. Their apparitions are frequently attended by the fall of meteorites, but more often they disappear after a series of loud detonations or a single violent explosion.   .

Shooting stars are meteors which flash across the sky, remaining visible only for a very short time, never more than about a second, and then disappear completely. All classes of meteors, large and small alike, owe their light to incandescence. Coming from outer space, they reach the upper regions of our atmosphere at a velocity so great that the friction caused by their passage through the air is sufficient to raise their temperature enormously. The larger class after penetrating the atmosphere continue their passage through it for a considerable time, some, as we have seen, reaching the earth's surface. In the case of the smaller meteors or shooting stars, however, the high temperature produced by the resistance of the atmosphere, which they often traverse at the rate of 30 to 40 miles a second, is sufficient to consume them in a moment. The average rate at which meteors speed through the air has been found to be about 25 or 26 miles a second. This is a greater speed than that at which the earth moves in its orbit, namely, 19 miles a second.

From constant observation it has been found that at least a few meteors are to be seen on any fine night. It is evident that a larger number of meteors will encounter the atmosphere on that side of the earth which faces the direction in which the earth is moving, than on the opposite side. In fig. 39 the arrows show the direction of the earth's motion in its orbit, and of its rotation on its axis, r being the point where sunrise is about to take place, and s the point where

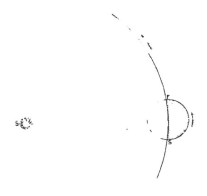

FIG. 39.

the sun is setting. We should expect on a general average more meteors at r than at s, that is, more in the morning than in the evening. But dawn to a great extent interferes with the observation of meteors, while darkness is favourable to their visibility. Hence we must look for the maximum number of meteors not at sunrise but some hours before dawn. Observation has shown that more are to be seen between 2 and 3 A.M. than at any other hour. It has been estimated that the number of meteors which invade our atmosphere every twenty-four hours must amount to several millions. Though separately each meteor must be of small dimensions, the smaller weighing probably no more than a few grains, yet in the aggregate their mass must be considerable.

Within the past half century the study of meteoric phenomena has engaged much attention. It has been shown that on certain nights of each year many more meteors are to be seen than the average number, and occasionally on these dates the number is so great as to constitute a "meteoric shower." The direction of a meteor's apparent flight in the sky is readily determined

by the position amongst the stars of the beginning and end of its path.
Observation of a meteoric shower consists: (1) in charting the apparent paths
of as many as possible on a map on which the positions of the brighter stars
have been laid down ; (2) in counting the numbers of individual meteors seen

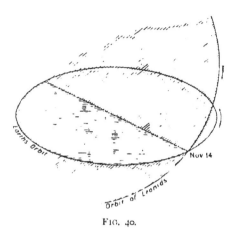

FIG. 40.

per minute at different times during the continuance of the shower. From
the former of these observations, an example of which appears on Plate X.,
it has been proved that the direction of apparent flight of the meteors in any
shower is away from a certain point in the sky called the "radiant point" of

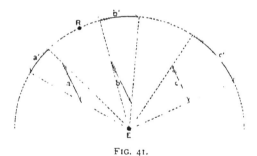

FIG. 41.

that shower. Some of the apparent paths of the meteors are short, and
close up to the radiant point, others are farther away and usually longer.
Continued observation of these radiant points from year to year has supplied
data from which it has been shown that the meteors forming the showers
travel in orbits under the all-pervading influence of the sun's attraction.
The same, doubtless, is true of those that appear separately, not apparently

belonging to any well-determined radiant point, or sporadic meteors, as they are called. The orbits of a number of the principal showers have been computed, and it has been shown that in many instances they are so like those of certain of the periodic comets, that no reasonable doubt can be entertained of the existence of a connection of some sort with the comets in whose orbits they have been found to travel. The comet of 1866, Tempel's, is thus associated with the Leonid meteors which appear on 14th November, and are so called because their radiant point is situated in the constellation Leo. The Perseid meteors, whose radiant is in the constellation Perseus, and which appear for several nights before and after 10th August, are similarly associated with Swift's comet of 1862. The shower radiating from Andromeda on 23rd and 24th November travels in the orbit of Biela's comet.

As we have seen, a shower of shooting stars consists of a number of small meteors moving together in a swarm in an orbit about the sun. In order that they may penetrate our atmosphere and become visible to us, it is necessary that the earth's orbit should be intersected by the meteoric orbit. In fig. 40 part of the orbit of the Leonids is shown crossing our orbit at the point where the earth is on 14th November. The meteors moving in parallel lines in their orbit become incandescent on encountering our atmosphere, and appear as bright streaks diverging from a point on the sky. The divergence from the radiant point is due solely to the effect of perspective. Fig. 41 illustrates the real and apparent paths of a meteoric shower. The real paths are shown by the parallel lines, a, b, and c. The appearances they present projected by perspective on the celestial vault and seen by an observer at E, are shown at a^1, b^1, and c^1. The three meteors a, b, and c are necessarily in the plane of the paper. Others of the shower will, of course, move in different planes, but all, as seen from E, will appear in the sky, on great circles of the celestial sphere, passing through the radiant point R.

From many of the known radiants showers reappear year after year at the same date, showing that the meteors are spread along the entire length of the orbit with some degree of uniformity. Such is the case with the August meteors, the Perseids. Every year when the earth reaches the point of intersection of its orbit with the Perseid orbit, on 10th August, we encounter a number of these meteors, resulting in a shower of greater or less persistence. A number of Perseids are also to be seen for a few days before and after this date, owing to the meteors not being collected into a thin stream in the immediate neighbourhood of the linear or theoretical orbit, but spread out for hundreds of miles on each side of it. The Leonids, on the other hand, appear as conspicuous showers only at intervals of several years, though a few members of the swarm are to be seen every year at the date of the shower, 14th November. From this it is evident that the Leonid meteors are thickly congregated along a part of their orbit only, the rest of the orbit being but sparsely populated. The crowded portion is probably long enough to occupy two or three years in passing any particular point of the orbit. The shower may therefore recur two or three years in succession, after which it will not be conspicuous for thirty-three or thirty-four years, thirty-three and a quarter years being the periodic time of the meteors. Their orbit is a very eccentric one, reaching out beyond the orbit of Uranus.

A large number of radiant points have been determined with great accuracy.

The following list gives the dates of a few of the most important showers, with the constellations in which their radiant points are situated.

Date.	Radiant.	
2nd and 3rd January . .	Draco-Hercules .	Annual shower, with long paths.
20th to 22nd April . .	Lyra . . .	Rapid meteors.
1st to 6th May . . .	Aquarius . . .	Orbit same as Halley's comet.
25th to 31st July . .	Aquarius . . .	Annual shower, with long paths.
10th to 12th August . .	Perseus . . .	Rich annual showers.
18th to 20th October . .	Orion . . .	Annual shower of swift meteors.
14th to 16th November .	Leo . . .	Fine displays in 1833 and 1866.
17th to 23rd November .	Andromeda . .	Biela's comet, slow meteors.
10th to 12th December .	Gemini . . .	Annual shower of short meteors.

Brief mention may here be made of two somewhat obscure phenomena of the solar system. The Zodiacal Light, an illustration of which will be found on Plate III., is a faintly luminous appearance seen stretching from the western horizon high up into the sky about half an hour after twilight from February to April, and before dawn on the eastern horizon from about August to October. Its origin is not very clearly understood, but as its axis appears to lie in the ecliptic, it is generally supposed to be due to sunlight reflected from minute meteoric particles crowding the region between the sun and the orbit of Mercury, and stretching out even as far as beyond the orbit of Venus. In tropic latitudes, where the ecliptic rises high above the horizon, the phenomenon is easily observed in clear skies all the year round. The Gegenschein, or Zodiacal counterglow, was discovered in 1854. It is an exceedingly faint diffused light seen in the part of the sky opposite the sun. Its cause has not yet received any satisfactory explanation.

CHAPTER XIV.

THE STARS.

THE number of stars visible to the naked eye on a fine clear night appears at first sight to be so great that any attempt to number them would seem to the ordinary observer to be an impossibility. That this is an erroneous idea the observer will soon find out for himself if he makes the attempt to count the number of separately distinct stars he can see in any small clearly defined portion of the sky. Argelander, the great German astronomer, devoted much attention to this point, and came to the conclusion that the number of stars in both hemispheres visible to the naked eye of an observer gifted with keen vision does not exceed 6000. When the telescope is brought to the assistance of the human eye it is found that a vast multitude of stars previously invisible come into view, and the number increases greatly with every increase in the optical power of the instrument.

The stars have been classified according to their brightness, the different classes being denoted by numbers, called their magnitudes. Thus about twenty of the brightest of the stars are said to be of the first magnitude. Then follow the second, third, fourth, fifth, and sixth magnitudes, the last including all the least bright stars visible to the naked eye of a person gifted with ordinarily good eyesight, and under average atmospheric conditions. This system of classification, which has been extended to the telescopic stars down to the fifteenth or sixteenth magnitudes, was found sufficient till the requirements of modern astronomical research, especially perhaps the investigation into the variability of the brightness of some of the stars, showed the necessity for introducing greater accuracy. This was done by sub-dividing the magnitudes into tenths. Thus we speak of stars of the 3·2 magnitude, 5·6 magnitude, 9·5 magnitude, and so on. It has been found that a typical star of the first magnitude is 100 times as bright as one of the sixth magnitude, and similarly a star of any magnitude is 100 times as bright as one five magnitudes less bright. From this it follows that the number two and a half can be adopted as the approximate *light ratio* for stars differing by one magnitude. The ratio is more accurately 2·5119. An average first magnitude star is two and a half times as bright as a second magnitude, and a fifth magnitude two and a half times as bright as a sixth magnitude, the same ratio being carried down through the telescopic stars. From the value of the light ratio for one magnitude it can easily be calculated that the light ratio for a tenth of a magnitude is 1·0965, or one and a tenth approximately, so that a star of the 3·2 magnitude is one and a tenth as bright as a star of the 3·3 magnitude. Only four or five of the twenty stars which for ages have been classed as of the first magnitude can, strictly speaking, be claimed as nearly equal in brightness to a typical or average first, the others being some brighter, some less bright than a first magnitude. As the numbers expressing magnitude *increase* with diminishing brightness, it is necessary to use 0, and even numbers with the minus sign, for the stars which are brighter than the first magnitude. In the same way the photometric magnitude of the sun, moon, and the bright planets can be expressed by minus numbers. The following list gives the photometric magnitudes of the sun, full moon, and the first magnitude stars, and their brightness compared with that of Aldebaran taken as unit :—

Name.	Magnitude.	Brightness.	Name.	Magnitude.	Brightness.
Sun	− 26·5	—	β Centauri . . .	0·7	1·3
Full Moon . . .	12·0	—	α Orionis, Betelguese .	0·9	1·1
Venus	− 3·0	39·8	α₁ Crucis . . .	0·9	1·1
α Canis Majoris, Sirius .	− 1·4	9·1	α Aquilæ, Altair .	0·9	1·1
α Argûs, Canopus . .	− 0·8	5·2	α Tauri, Aldebaran .	1·0	1·0
α Aurigæ, Capella . .	0·1	2·3	α Virginis, Spica .	1·1	0·9
α Boötis, Arcturus . .	0·2	2·1	β Geminorum, Pollux .	1·2	0·8
α₂ Centauri . . .	0·2	2·1	α Scorpii, Antares .	1·2	0·8
α Lyræ, Vega . . .	0·2	2·1	α Leonis, Regulus .	1·3	0·8
β Orionis, Rigel .	0·3	1·9	α Piscis Australis, Fomal-		
α Eridani, Achernar .	0·4	1·7	haut . . .	1·3	0·8
α Canis Minoris, Procyon	0·5	1·6	α Cygni, Deneb . .	1·4	0·7

The sun is thus 14·5 magnitudes brighter than the full moon, and 27·5 magnitudes brighter than Aldebaran ; or, in absolute brightness, the sun is 631,000 times as bright as the full moon, and more than 100,000,000,000 times as bright as a typical first magnitude star.

The colour of a majority of the stars, including many of the brightest, is white. A large number also are of a yellow or orange hue, and others are distinctly red. The contrast of colours will be clearly seen by comparing the red star Betelguese with any of the other bright stars in the constellation Orion, or the red Aldebaran with Sirius. To appreciate the contrast fully a red star and a white one should be looked at alternately several times in succession. The number of green or blue stars is small, and those that exist are always to be found as one component of a double star. Some good examples of the contrasted colours of doubles will be found on Plate IX.

Of double stars there are two distinct kinds—optical doubles and binary stars. In the optical doubles the components have no physical connection with one another but are simply placed so nearly in the same line of sight, that to the naked eye they look like one star, and it requires some amount of telescopic aid to show them separately. One of the components may, however, be many millions of miles farther away from us than the other. In the binary stars the two components are bound together by the force of attraction, so that the smaller star revolves about the other, or more strictly speaking they both revolve about their common centre of gravity. Graphic representations of the orbits of two well-known binaries will be found on Plate IX. The companion, or smaller star, in the case of ζ Herculis revolves completely round the principal star in thirty-five years. The binary γ Virginis was seen as a double star by Bradley in 1718.

The components are both of about the third magnitude, and revolve about their common centre of gravity in 170 years. In their revolution they appear to approach one another, till the two stars are seen as one. This happened in 1836, since which date they have been again separating. They are now so far apart as to be easily seen double with a small telescope. A few multiple stars are known, such as ζ Cancri, a triple, consisting of a close double with a more distant companion, and ε Lyræ, a quadruple. With a very small telescope the latter is seen as a double, but greater optical power shows that each of the components is itself a double. A still larger instrument will show two or three very minute stars in the space between the two doubles.

Many of the stars have been found to be of variable brightness, their lustre passing through cycles of variability of more or less regularity in certain definite periods. The most remarkable known variable is perhaps ο Ceti, known as Mira. The period of its variability is 331 days 8 hours, during which it fades from the second magnitude till it becomes about equal in brightness to its small companion of the ninth magnitude. At its maximum it is, therefore, about 600 times as bright as at its minimum. It remains invisible to the naked eye for about five months in each of its cycles. In colour it is deep red. It is very irregular in its changes, being at maximum sometimes no brighter than between the third and fourth magnitudes. Its period is also irregular. Mira has been known as a variable for at least two and a half centuries. The researches of Sir Wm. Herschel added much to our knowledge of its changes. Variables with periods of change of brightness not exceeding one month are known as short period variables. A large number of these are of the class of which Algol, or β Persei, is the type. In this class the star remains at its maximum brightness for the greater part of its cycle, its change of lustre occupying usually only a few hours. Algol is generally seen as a star of the second magnitude, but decreases to a 3·5 magnitude, and brightens again to its normal magnitude in about seven hours. At this it remains for over two and a half days, the complete cycle of its variability being 2 days 20 hours 49 minutes. In the Algol type of variable it is now generally believed that the decrease of light is caused by eclipse. Each of them is a binary, with a darker star for its companion. In each revolution of the components about one another the darker star intervenes between us and the bright one, thus for a short time eclipsing a considerable portion of the light of the latter. In the case of a number of variables of this class it is supposed that irregularities which have been observed in the length of their periods and in their brightness may be accounted for by the existence of two or even more satellites less bright than the principal star.

There is a second class of short period variables of the β Lyræ type, in which the time of both the maximum and minimum of brightness may be observed with some exactness. β Lyræ varies from a maximum of 3·4 magnitude to a minimum of about 4·5 magnitude in 9 days 20 hours, and returns to its maximum brightness in 3 days 2 hours, the alternate minima being slightly unequal. Some stars of this class have secondary maxima and minima. All stars whose changes of brightness occupy longer than one month are known as long period variables. A large proportion of these have periods of about one year, and with a very few known exceptions their periods do not exceed some two years. Recent research appears to assign to the star ε Aurigæ a period of about twenty-seven years, and to η Carinæ, a star with very irregular fluctuations of brightness, a still

H

longer period. The former varies from 3·0 magnitude to 4·5 magnitude; the latter, a brilliant first magnitude star at its maximum, fades at minimum to a 7·6 magnitude, but only long continued observation can fix the period in such cases with certainty. The list of variable stars includes nearly 600 with known periods, and some 500 the periods of which are still undetermined. There are, besides, many variables situated in the star clusters.

Temporary stars, or Novæ, may be looked upon as a class of variables of very long period, but of quite a different character from the two classes just referred to. They appear suddenly in the sky, and after a time disappear altogether, or become so diminished in brightness as to be visible only in large telescopes. One of these objects is said to have appeared in the time of Hipparchus, and to have suggested to him the idea of preparing a catalogue of all the stars visible to the naked eye. The first Nova of which we have any authentic account was discovered by Tycho Brahe in 1572. It remained visible for seventeen months, and at its maximum brightness was compared to Venus at her greatest brilliancy. The two most interesting Novæ of late years were discovered by an Edinburgh astronomer, one in the constellation Auriga in 1892, and the other in Perseus in 1901. On Plate IX. the position of the Nova of 1901 is shown, from a photograph of part of the constellation Perseus. The Nova has been surrounded by a small circle. Both these Novæ have been studied with the aid of the spectroscope by astronomers in all parts of the world. Their spectra showed both dark and bright lines of the same chemical substances, the dark lines being displaced by a small amount towards one end of the spectrum, and the bright lines towards the other end. The explanation of these displacements given by many scientists is that the sudden outburst of light was due to the collision of two bodies moving in opposite directions, probably a hitherto invisible star with a nebula.

Nova Auriga was of 4·5 magnitude in February 1892 when first seen. Early in March it began to fade, and by the end of that month was only a twelfth magnitude. In August it increased in brilliancy to the ninth magnitude, only to fade away a few months later to less than the fifteenth magnitude. Nova Persei when first seen, 21st February 1901, was of 2·7 magnitude, and increased two days after its discovery to brighter than a first magnitude, rivalling Capella in brilliancy; by the month of April it had diminished to a fifth magnitude, and in a few months later it was only of the 11·5 magnitude. In July 1893, at Harvard College, U.S.A., a Nova of the seventh magnitude was discovered in the constellation Norma. Still more recently, March 1903, another Nova was discovered by Professor Turner in the constellation Gemini, close to the borders of Auriga, on a photograph made at the University Observatory, Oxford.

Of the clusters of stars a few only are visible as separate stars to the naked eye. Two of these, the Pleiades and Hyades, are in the constellation Taurus. The cluster Præsepe in Cancer can hardly be said to be resolvable into distinct stars by the naked eye, except on fine dark nights and to keen sight. The constellation Coma Berenicis, situated above Virgo, may also be considered a naked eye cluster. The great majority of these objects require more or less telescopic assistance to separate them into stars. Some have never been separated even in the most powerful telescopes, though the spectroscope has proved them to consist of stars. Plate IX. gives a view of the cluster in Hercules, discovered by Halley in 1714. Herschel estimated the number of stars in this cluster to be not less than 14,000. The double cluster in the "sword-hand" of Perseus, also shown on

Plate IX., is a good example of an object of this class, which is resolvable into distinct stars by small telescopic power. Both have been reproduced from photographs made at the Royal Observatory, Edinburgh.

Under the term Nebulæ is generally included both the gaseous nebulæ and all those objects which have never been resolved by the most powerful telescopes, though in many cases the spectroscope has shown them to be clusters of stars. They have been classified according to their appearance in the telescope into annular, elliptic, spiral and planetary nebulæ, and nebulous stars. A few of the most interesting of these objects are the Ring Nebula in Lyra, the only annular nebula visible in ordinary telescopes, shown by its spectrum to be a ring of luminous gas; the very curious Nebula in Cygnus, composed of numerous wisps of luminous matter; the Great Nebula in Orion, visible to the naked eye and showing wonderful details in moderate sized telescopes; the Great Nebula in Andromeda, and the Spiral Nebula in Canes Venatici, both shown by the spectroscope to be of a stellar character, though in neither case has any sign of resolvability into distinct stars been seen in the largest telescopes. The Orion Nebula has been proved to be of a gaseous nature. The spectra of nebulæ usually show three characteristic rays in spectroscopes of moderate power, one of which coincides with the blue line of hydrogen. Other hydrogen lines are also sometimes seen, but much less bright. Certain nebulæ also show other bright lines, such as the yellow helium line, discovered by Professor Copeland in 1888 in the spectrum of the Great Nebula in Orion.

The methods by which the distances of the sun and moon from the earth have been measured have been already referred to. Various attempts made to measure the distances of the stars failed in obtaining any certain result, till in 1837 the German astronomer Bessel succeeded in securing a trustworthy value for the parallax of the star known as 61 Cygni. Soon after this the late Thomas Henderson, Astronomer Royal for Scotland, measured the parallax of the southern star α Centauri. In both cases the diameter of the earth's orbit is used as the base line, and the method depends on the possibility of measuring the apparent angular displacement of the star whose distance is sought, with reference to a star seen close to it, nearly in the same line of sight, but much farther away in actual distance. So far it has been found that a very few only of the stars show any sign of this parallactic displacement when viewed from opposite ends of a diameter of the earth's orbit. In all cases where the attempt has been made it has been shown that, with these few exceptions, the distances of the stars are so great that the whole expanse of the earth's orbit is a mere point in comparison. Bessel's value of the parallax of 61 Cygni was 0.34″; in other words, he found that the radius of the earth's orbit would subtend that very small angle at the distance of 61 Cygni. Similarly, Henderson's value for the parallax of α Centauri was nearly 1″. More recent investigations, however, have brought out slightly different values. These are, for 61 Cygni 0.30″, and for α Centauri 0.76″, values which signify that the former star is situated at a distance from our solar system of 64,000,000,000,000 miles, and the latter at a distance of 25,000,000,000,000 miles. Till recently α Centauri was supposed to be the nearest to us of all the fixed stars, but measurements of a star, of about the eleventh magnitude, close to α, show that this small star is somewhat nearer to us, and it has been appropriately named *Proxima*. The distances of the stars are so great that, even in the case of nearest, it is impossible for the human mind to form any conception of them when expressed as a number of miles. The convenient method has been adopted of stating the distances with reference to the "light-year" as a unit. The light-year is simply the distance over which light will travel in one year. It is known that light takes 8 minutes 18 seconds to reach us from the sun. If this number of seconds be divided into the number of seconds in a year it will be found that light will travel over 63,290 times the distance between sun and earth in one year, or 63,290 × 92,897,000 miles. This distance is known as the light-year. From this value, and the distance of α Centauri and 61 Cygni given above, it follows that light takes nearly four and a half years to reach us from the former star, and nearly eleven to reach us from the latter. The following list contains a few of the stars whose distances have been measured, with their parallax and distance in light years :—

Star.	*Parallax.*	*Distance in Light-Years.*	*Star.*	*Parallax.*	*Distance in Light-Years.*
	"				
Proxima Centauri .	0·79	4·1	η Cassiopeiæ .	0·21	15 5
α Centauri . .	0·76	4·3	Aldebaran . .	0·15	21·7
Sirius . . .	0·38	8·6	Vega . . .	0·12	27·2
61 Cygni .	0·30	10·9	Capella .	0·12	27·2
Procyon . .	0·30	10·9	Polaris . . .	0·07	46·5
Altair . . .	0·22	14·8			

Besides the stars in the above table, the parallax and distance of several others have been determined with as much accuracy as the circumstances of such an investigation will admit of. It must be borne in mind that the angles to be measured are so small that their determination is a matter of extreme difficulty and delicacy. The values of the parallaxes must therefore be looked upon as subject to some uncertainty, and the distances derived from them as only approximate.

Proper motion is the name applied to a real movement of the stars in reference to one another, by which they undergo a slight change of place on the celestial sphere. They have for ages been called "fixed" stars, in contradistinction to the planets whose movements on the face of the sky become apparent in a very short time. The word "fixed" as applied to the stars must not be taken as implying that they are unaffected by any motion. This is far from being the case The effect of proper motion in altering the relative position of a star is, of course, measured in angle, and in a direction at right angles to the line of sight, and though of small annual amount, yet in the course of centuries it is sufficient to change the aspect of the constellations perceptibly. The spectroscope has revealed the second component of the proper motion of the stars—namely, their motion in the line of sight. This is made possible by the effect of motion on light to which Doppler called attention in 1842. It has been illustrated by the somewhat similar effect of motion on sound. When an express train is approaching a station sounding its whistle, the note heard by a person at rest in the station is of a higher pitch so long as the train is rushing towards the station than it is when the train is passing by, and it becomes of lower pitch when the movement is away from the station. Similarly, if a star is approaching the earth more waves of light are received every second in the eye of an observer than if the star and earth were at rest. Consequently, the wave-length appears to be shortened, and when the star's light is analysed by the spectroscope the lines of its spectrum appear to be of shorter wave-length than they would be under normal conditions, and are slightly shifted towards the violet end of the spectrum. On the other hand, if the star were receding from us fewer waves of light would be received per second, and the waves would appear to be longer. The lines of the spectrum would then appear of greater wave-length, or shifted towards the red. The measurement of these slight displacements in the lines of the spectra of many stars has shown that some of them are approaching us, and many others receding from us, with motions differing largely for individual stars, and in some cases reaching as much as 50 miles a second. Thus, Aldebaran is receding from us at the rate of about 30 miles a second, and Rigel at about 13 miles a second; while γ Leonis is approaching us at 25 miles a second, and Spica at about 10 miles a second. Recent researches into the proper motions of the stars have shown that the whole of this movement is not due to the motions of the stars themselves, but that part of it is the result of the parallactic displacement arising from a movement of the sun and its attendant planets through space. The direction of the sun's motion in space has been found to be towards a point on the borders of the constellations Lyra and Hercules, not far from the star Vega. This point is known as the "apex of the sun's way." The sun is thus shown to have itself a proper motion. For this and other reasons the sun must be looked upon as being itself a star, and the so-called "fixed" stars as suns, our luminary being but a unit in the vast host of heaven.

Spectroscopic study of the light of the stars has shown that at least the brightest of them exist in a physical condition somewhat similar to that of our sun. This interesting research has been prosecuted with much vigour during the second half of the nineteenth century by many physicists, amongst whom we need mention only the names of Secchi, Vogel, Huggins, Miller, Janssen, and Lockyer. As soon as the spectra of a large number of stars had been studied it was seen that they differed considerably from one another, though all were alike in showing that the light of the brighter stars emanates from bodies in a state of intense incandescence surrounded by atmospheres, consisting of vapours capable of absorbing portions of the light. About 1866 Secchi made the first classification of the stars into types according to their spectra. He recognised four types, each embracing spectra with similar characteristic features. His first type consists of stars the spectra of which are continuous from the red to the violet, but are always crossed by four broad dark lines of hydrogen, one in the red, one in the bluish-green, and two in the violet, and sometimes also by a number of fine lines. Most of the spectra of the white stars belong to this class—those of Sirius, Vega, Altair, Rigel, for example. This is the most numerous class, nearly half the stars hitherto examined being included in it.

The second type, to which our sun belongs, includes the yellow or orange stars, such as Arcturus, Aldebaran, Procyon, and Alpha Ursæ Majoris. The spectra of this class are characterised by the large number of fine dark lines which cross them, and they closely resemble the solar spectrum.

The third type of spectra is characterised by dark bands, sharp and well defined on the side towards the blue end of the spectrum, and shaded off gradually towards the red. The red stars are of this class, including Alpha Orionis, Alpha Herculis, and Antares.

The fourth type of spectra is given by a comparatively small number of stars of a deep red colour. The characteristic feature of these spectra consists of bands shading off towards the blue, and sharp on the side towards the red.

A fifth type of spectra has more recently been added. It consists of spectra containing both bright lines and dark bands. The stars showing spectra of this type are known as Wolf-Rayet stars, from two astronomers of the Paris Observatory, to whose investigations our knowledge of this class of stars is due. The Wolf-Rayet stars are less than a hundred in number, and are nearly all situated near the central line of the "Milky Way."

Other classifications of the stars by their spectra have been made, but that of Secchi has been probably most widely adopted. Many stars show peculiar spectra which cannot be included in any of the above types.

Plates XI. to XVI. are devoted to a set of maps of the stars, constructed on the gnomonic projection of the sphere. The catalogue of stars published by the British Association for the Advancement of Science has been adopted as the authority in laying down the positions of the stars. The maps include all stars down to the 5·5 magnitude. Nebulæ and clusters are marked *Neb. Var.* signifies that the object is a variable star ; and *Nova* indicates a new or temporary star. In addition to these, six smaller maps have been introduced into the text, showing interesting portions of the sky. They are intended to enable the student to see at a glance the relative positions and configuration of the more striking constellations, and to fix in the mind the positions of various objects of interest, so as to enable him to locate them on the sky without difficulty. The position of nebulæ, clusters, and novæ are indicated by a small circle.

Fig. 42 shows the northern circumpolar constellations. The months, as well as the hours of right ascension, have been placed round the edge, so that the map may be turned round till it shows the position of the constellations at midnight at any time of the year approximately. This is done by holding the map with the month uppermost, and with its back to the north. The most prominent constellation in this map is Ursa Major, the "Great Bear." Besides the region marked out by its seven brightest stars, known as the "Plough," sometimes also as the "Dipper," Ursa Major stretches over a large area, which may be readily made out on the sky by looking for three pairs of fourth magnitude stars, forming the paws of the bear, as represented on celestial globes. One pair consists of the stars ι and κ, the second of λ and μ, and the third of ν and ξ. The last pair must be looked for on fig. 44. The star ζ, in the handle of the Plough, is known as Mizar. and with Alcor forms a pair easily separated by the naked eye. Mizar is itself a telescopic double, having a pale green companion of about 4·2 magnitude. Of

the seven brightest stars of the Plough, five have proper motions in the same
direction, and of nearly the same amount, while α and η have a proper motion in
the opposite direction. These movements, though slight, are sufficient sensibly to
alter to the eye the relative positions of these stars after the lapse of several
centuries. A number of interesting nebulæ will be found within the body
of the Plough. The most southern of those shown in fig. 42 is a planetary
nebula. In the upper part of the constellation, near the borders of Draco,

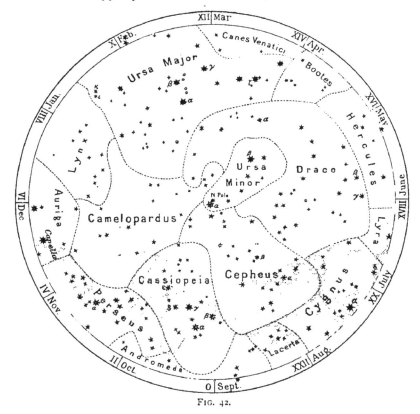

FIG. 42.

another fine nebula is to be seen. It has been shown by the spectroscope
to be not of a gaseous nature, but really a cluster of stars, though it has
never been resolved into distinct stars by the telescope.

A line drawn from β to α of the Great Bear and produced will pass close
to the Pole Star, and if produced as far again, will just miss the constellation
Cassiopeia. In fig. 42 there is shown the position in this constellation of Tycho
Brahe's Nova of 1572. It forms the northern corner of a diamond-shaped
figure, of which the other corners are α, β, and γ. Near β the place is marked
of a fine cluster discovered by Caroline Herschel in 1783. It consists of a

large number of minute stars. Between δ and ε another fine cluster is marked
containing stars of various magnitudes.

The constellation Cepheus lies between Cassiopeia and Draco, and stretches
from near the Pole Star to Cygnus. It contains no very conspicuous stars,
but a small telescope will show many groups, especially about α, in the southern
part of the constellation, where it is crossed by the Milky Way. The star
β is a fine double, the larger component white, and of the third magnitude,
with a blue companion of the eighth magnitude.

Draco is an extensive constellation, but the stream of fairly bright stars
of which it is composed to the naked eye can be traced easily. The head of

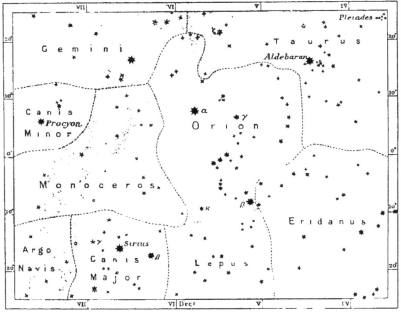

Fig. 43.

the dragon lies on the borders of Hercules, and is formed of three stars—γ, a
second magnitude, and β and ξ, two third magnitudes. These with ι Herculis
form a diamond-shaped figure. The broadest part of the constellation lies
between Cygnus and Ursa Minor, and from this the stream of stars can be
followed round to the opposite side of the Pole. α Draconis lies about half-
way between the handle of the Plough and β Ursæ Minoris. A line drawn
from ι Herculis to ξ Draconis, the long diameter of the diamond, and produced
nearly as far again will show a beautiful planetary nebula, the spectrum of
which is gaseous.

Camelopardus lies at the opposite side of the Pole Star from the broadest part of Draco. The constellation is not easily traced, but a line drawn from Capella to the Pole passes nearly through the middle of it.

Perseus can be found easily from its proximity to Cassiopeia. The chief part of this constellation consists of the festoon of crowded stars stretching from Cassiopeia to near Capella, the bright star in Auriga. A splendid double cluster, visible to the naked eye, lies at the upper end of the festoon, near the borders of Cassiopeia ; a line from γ Cassiopeia to δ points to it. On celestial globes the cluster forms the "sword-hand" of Perseus. A photograph of the cluster is reproduced on Plate IX.

In fig. 42 the Milky Way is shown passing through the constellations Cygnus, Cepheus, Cassiopeia, and Perseus. Here, as in other parts of the Galaxy, will be found a profusion of stellar groups and configurations of interest to the possessor of a small telescope.

Fig. 43 shows the constellation Orion and its surroundings, one of the most interesting portions of the sky to British observers, being visible during the winter months at a fair altitude in the early hours of the night. The figure contains no fewer than five of the first magnitude stars given in the list on p. 112.

Orion is itself a splendid constellation, and contains many objects of interest to be seen with the assistance of a small telescope. Two of its stars are of the first magnitude—α, or Betelguese, and β, or Rigel. The latter is considerably brighter than the former, and is white in colour, with perhaps a slight yellow tinge. Betelguese is a variable with an irregular period, its limits of variability being from 1·0 to 1·4 magnitude. In colour it is red, in strong contrast to the other bright stars of the constellation. The three stars in the belt are called δ, ϵ, and ζ. The uppermost star on the right, δ, is a double, a second magnitude with a seventh magnitude companion, and lies just south of the equator. The star on the left, ζ, is a triple, a 3·0 magnitude, with companions of the 6·5 and 10·0 magnitudes. The sword, or dagger, of Orion is made up, to the naked eye, of three stars in a north and south line, the uppermost of the fifth magnitude, and the others of the fourth and third respectively. The middle one of them, known as θ, is involved in the densest part of that most wonderful object, the "Great Nebula in Orion." The nebula is visible to the naked eye as a cloudy mass, and even a small telescope will show some of its details. Larger instruments are necessary if it is desired to see all its branches and loops. Many beautiful drawings have been made of this nebula, the finest of which is probably that made by the late Lord Rosse, with the assistance of his great reflecting telescope. Analysis of its light by the spectroscope has shown that it is a mass of glowing gases—hydrogen, and some others. Many other interesting objects will be found in this constellation by the careful observer. In the very northernmost part of the constellation is the place in which a Nova appeared in 1885.

The constellation Taurus is conspicuously marked by its leading star Aldebaran and by the two well-known groups, the Pleiades and Hyades. Both these groups are interesting when viewed with low powers. In the Pleiades six stars are quite obvious to the unaided eye any clear night. Glimpses of several others may be had on favourable nights with good eyesight. The telescope will show about 400 stars down to the fourteenth magnitude, and many less bright. The brightest star in the group, named Alcyone, has a triangle of three small stars close to it. A map of the group is given on Plate IX. with the names of the principal stars. Photographs of the group have shown that some of the principal stars are surrounded by nebulæ.

The Crab Nebula lies north-west of the star ζ Tauri, known as the bull's southern horn.

Canis Major is a small constellation, but remarkable in its possession of the brightest of all the fixed stars. Sirius has a small companion of the tenth magnitude, visible only in large telescopes. South of Sirius, nearly in

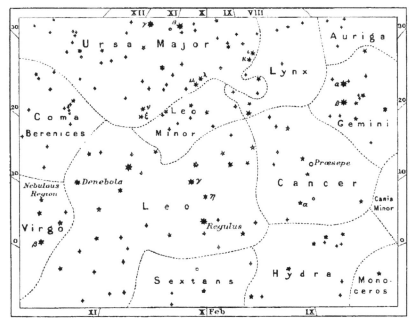

Fig. 44.

the centre of the constellation, is a splendid cluster visible to the naked eye. A small telescope is sufficient to separate many of its stars, which are of various magnitudes, the larger ones being arranged in curves. East of Sirius is another cluster of stars, nearly all of which are about the tenth magnitude.

In Canis Minor the chief object of interest is Procyon, a white or pale yellow star, with several small companions.

Monoceros is a very inconspicuous constellation to the naked eye, but its position is easily made out, as it borders on the east side of Orion, and occupies the space between Canis Major and Canis Minor. A brilliant part of the Milky Way passes through the constellation, and it contains some interesting clusters. Amongst these, one visible to the naked eye lies a little north of the line joining Betelguese to Procyon, about one-third of the distance from the former. It contains one sixth magnitude star, and a dense mass of smaller ones down to the fourteenth magnitude. Another cluster lies on the line between Procyon and Sirius, one-third of the distance from the latter. It is a straggling cluster of stars from eighth to thirteenth magnitude. One of its stars is red.

Fig. 44 shows Leo and the surrounding constellations. Leo is distinctly marked to the naked eye. The principal stars take the form of a "sickle," with three bright stars forming a triangle on the left. The lowest star of the " sickle " is Regulus, or Cor Leonis, the lion's heart, a first magnitude star with a small distant companion. The eastmost star of the triangle is Denebola, or β Leonis, a second magnitude with six small stars around it, one of which is a close double. The lowest star in the curve of the sickle is γ, said by Struve, the Russian astronomer, to be the most beautiful star in the northern heavens. It is a binary with a period of 407 years, the larger star of the pair being 2 magnitude and of a yellowish colour, the companion 3·5 magnitude and greenish-red in hue. The star ι below the triangle is a double, the components being 3·9 and 7·1 magnitudes, pale yellow and light blue in colour. Between this star and θ, at the right angle, are two rather faint but interesting nebulæ, one of which is a spiral. Almost on the line joining Regulus with Denebola, somewhat nearer the former, are several nebulæ, the brightest of which has a stellar nucleus. East of Denebola lies the nebulous region, roughly enclosed by this star and several bright stars in the upper part of the constellation Virgo. This region crosses the northern boundary of Virgo, and embraces nearly half of Coma Berenicis. It contains within its boundaries a larger number of nebulæ than are to be found in any equal area of the heavens.

The constellation Cancer contains the cluster known as Præsepe, or the bee-hive. On fine clear nights it is resolvable with the naked eye into separate stars. A small telescope will show some fine combinations.

The constellation Gemini is best known by its two brightest stars, Castor and Pollux. Pollux, a 1·1 magnitude, is the brighter, though Castor, a second magnitude, is dignified by being known as the α star of the constellation. A similar instance of this occurs in Orion, where the β star, Rigel, is much brighter than α, Betelguese. Gemini contains a large number of double stars, of which Castor is one. The components of the latter are of magnitudes 2 and 2·8, and form a binary system of long and uncertain period. They are both white, with perhaps a tinge of green, and are easily separated with a small telescope. This constellation extends to a considerable distance west and south of its two principal stars. Two of its bright stars, μ and ε, point out its western extension, where its boundaries reach the constellation Taurus, not far from the "horns of the Bull." Above these stars, and rather nearer to Taurus, lies a splendid cluster. Its brightest stars are of about the ninth magnitude, and distributed all over the cluster. In the telescope it will be seen to contain a large number of stars down to the faintest possible. Below Castor and Pollux, and a little east of the third magnitude star δ, are two interesting objects. One is a densely crowded cluster of very small stars. The other is a nebula with a stellar nucleus which the spectroscope has shown to be a mass of luminous gas.

The constellation Coma Berenicis, situated above Virgo and east of Leo, is of small dimensions, but contains the interesting group which forms the principal portion of the constellation as seen with the naked eye. To the possessor of a telescope the chief interest in this constellation lies in the numerous nebulæ and clusters with which it abounds. At least two will be found on the east side of the bright group; one is a long faint streak with a small stellar nucleus, another is condensed towards the centre, and fairly bright.

Fig. 45 shows Boötes, Hercules, and the neighbouring constellations.

The principal star of Boötes is Arcturus. It stands fourth on the list of the brightest stars on p. 112. In colour it is reddish-yellow or orange. It has a large annual proper motion at right angles to the line of sight, which would

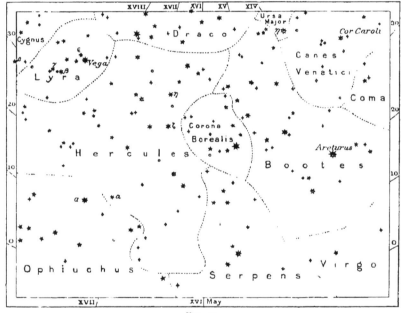

FIG. 45.

lead to the supposition that it might be one of the stars with a large parallax, and therefore one of the nearest to us. This, however, is not quite the case, for though its parallax is measurable it is small, and the star therefore at an immense distance from us. Its light takes more than twenty-five years to reach the earth. Its actual motion must therefore be enormous. In confirmation of this it has been found spectroscopically that it is moving in our direction at the rate of 55 miles per second. Boötes contains a large number of doubles, but few clusters and nebulæ. The most remarkable of the doubles is ε. Its components are a 3 magnitude, yellow in colour, and a 5 magnitude, blue. The colours are well contrasted, and the object is an easy one for small telescopes. It lies nearly north-east of Arcturus, and has a fifth magnitude star close to it. A good idea of the contrasted colours may be seen on Plate IX. The constellation reaches in a northerly direction, between Corona Borealis and Canes Venatici, as far as the star η Ursæ Majoris in the tip of the Bear's tail, where its highest point is marked by three fourth magnitude stars, two of which are doubles

Corona Borealis lies between Boötes and Hercules, and to the naked eye appears as a semicircle of bright stars, with the brightest half way along the curve. It contains a number of double and variable stars, but the most interesting object in the constellation is the Nova discovered by Mr Birmingham, of Tuam, in 1866. The star is set down in the Bonn catalogue of 1855 as a 9·5 magnitude. A few hours before Mr Birmingham's discovery it was certainly not visible to the naked eye. On 12th May he was surprised to find it suddenly enlarged to a second magnitude. It soon, however, began to decline, and had returned to about its original magnitude by the middle of June. This was the first temporary star which it was possible to examine with the spectroscope. In addition to Secchi's third type of spectrum it showed a number of the bright lines of hydrogen, to an outburst of which its increase of brilliancy was possibly due.

Hercules is a widespread constellation lying under the head of Draco and between Lyra and Corona Borealis. It reaches south nearly to the equator. It is uninteresting to the naked eye, but contains a number of beautiful telescopic objects. Its brightest star, α, in the head of the figure of Hercules on globes, is a double, with components 3·5 and 5·5 magnitudes, orange and bluish-green respectively. Close by it, a little to the left, is the chief star of Ophiuchus, the Serpent Bearer. The most interesting object in Hercules is probably the wonderful globular cluster shown on Plate IX. It lies between the stars η and ζ Herculis, and nearly half-way between α Coronæ and Vega, rather nearer the former. A moderate telescope will show it dotted with stars of the tenth to the fifteenth magnitudes, or possibly smaller. Many of its stars are arranged in spiral curves. The Earl of Rosse discovered three dark " lanes " or rifts in the compact mass of stars, meeting at a point within the body of the cluster. These markings are well shown by photography, but are not easily reproduced in engravings. North-east of η Herculis is another fine cluster, easily seen with a small telescope, in which it looks like a nebula, a moderately sized instrument being required to resolve it into stars. It is much condensed and very bright in the centre, and this part can be separated into distinct stars only by powerful telescopes. A fine planetary nebula will be found by drawing a line from η Herculis to ζ, and producing it as far again. It is slightly bluish in colour, and has a gaseous spectrum.

Lyra is a small constellation lying between Cygnus and Hercules, but containing, for its size, a large number of interesting objects. Its chief star, Vega, a first magnitude, has a minute companion, not easily seen owing to the brightness of the primary. The star ε, situated to the left of Vega, consists of two doubles, with three very minute stars between them. The slightest optical aid will show ε as a double, and a moderate instrument will show each of the components to be itself double. They are both binaries of long periods. Between the stars β and γ Lyræ lies the well-known annular, or ring-nebula, the only object of this class visible in moderate telescopes. Its spectrum, consisting of bright lines, proves it to be composed of incandescent gas. On the line from γ Lyræ to β Cygni, rather nearer the latter, is a globular cluster, a dense mass of stars.

Fig. 46 shows the constellations Cygnus and Pegasus and their surroundings.

Cygnus is almost entirely involved in the Milky Way, which, near the principal star, Deneb, divides into two streams. The brighter stars are in the form of a cross, having Deneb at the top, γ at the centre, and β at the foot. As will be seen from the list on p. 112, the magnitude of Deneb is given as 1·4 and its brightness therefore seven-tenths of that of a first magnitude star. β Cygni is a beautiful double star, the larger component is a third magnitude,

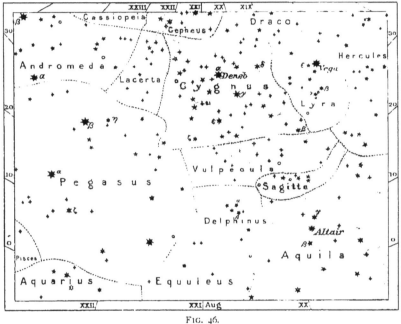

FIG. 46.

and reddish-yellow in colour, the smaller 5·3 magnitude, and blue. The larger is slightly variable in magnitude, and, it is said, also in colour. δ is a close double, with components third magnitude and 7·9, but the companion is difficult to see in telescopes of moderate power. Reference has already been made to 61 Cygni on p. 115. It is a double star, consisting of two yellow components of 5·3 and 5·9 magnitudes. To locate it on the sky, complete the parallelogram of which three of the angles are at the stars α, γ, and ε; the remaining angle will lie close to 61. Near the borders of Lacerta the position is marked on the figure of the Nova which suddenly appeared of the third magnitude in November 1876. By September of the following year it had faded to a 10·5 magnitude, and a year later it was only of the thirteenth or fourteenth magnitude.

Its spectrum at first showed the bright lines of hydrogen and a few other substances, but later was reduced to a single bright line, similar to the usual spectrum of a planetary nebula. The constellation Cygnus contains many magnificent groups of stars, and will repay examination with low powers. An interesting nebula is situated between the stars ε and ζ, on the borders of the Milky Way.

Pegasus is a widespread constellation, stretching from Andromeda southwards nearly to the equator. Its most conspicuous portion is easily recognised by the great square which three of its bright stars, α, β, and γ, make with the bright star in the head of Andromeda. Algenib, or γ Pegasi, does not appear in fig. 46, but will be found in the larger map on Plate XI. It is a 2·5 magnitude star reddish in colour, with two minute companions of about the eleventh magnitude. Slight changes of brilliancy have been noticed in β Pegasi, which also has a faint companion. The second magnitude star, ε, low down in the constellation, is a triple, one of its companions being ninth magnitude, and the other very minute, about fourteenth magnitude. The primary is yellow, the companions both blue. To the right of it the position of a beautiful globular cluster of stars is marked on fig. 46. A telescope of moderate size will show the edges of the cluster resolved into stars, but the centre is more condensed. A cluster of quite a different appearance from the last lies a little north of the line joining α with γ Pegasi, and about one-third of the distance from the latter star. It consists of widely scattered stars with no central condensation.

The constellation Andromeda, part of which is shown in fig. 46, contains many interesting objects, including many doubles, and some fine groups. The object of absorbing interest in this constellation is the "Great Nebula." Its position is shown on the figure near the star β. On fine dark nights it may be seen with the naked eye, and is quite easily visible in a binocular glass. A moderately sized telescope will show it as an irregularly oval nebula, bright towards the centre and fainter at the edges. The central condensation will be seen in larger telescopes surrounded by curves of nebulosity, conveying the idea of a spiral seen obliquely. No part of the nebula appears to have been with certainty resolved into stars, yet the spectrum is continuous, showing that the nebula is not gaseous, but a condensed cluster of stars. A companion nebula is also a cluster of stars, but is resolvable only in powerful telescopes. A small but bright planetary nebula, showing a spiral structure in large instruments, lies in the rough continuation of the curve formed by three fourth magnitude stars in the western part of Andromeda. Its disc is bluish in colour, and its spectrum consists of four bright lines, proving it to be certainly of a gaseous nature.

The constellation Vulpecula lies below Cygnus. Its chief object of interest is the "Dumb-bell" Nebula. Its position lies a few degrees above the east end of the line of small stars forming the constellation Sagitta. The nebula was so named by the late Lord Rosse, and in a fairly powerful telescope the two broader ends can be seen connected by a narrower portion, though the latter is so broad as to give the whole figure more the appearance of an ellipse. There are several stars scattered over the nebula. The spectroscope has shown it to be gaseous; the stars must therefore belong to the Milky Way.

The little constellation Sagitta is easily located on the sky from its position with reference to the three bright stars of Aquila. It contains two star clusters of interest—one in the middle of the row of stars forming the arrow, the other on the east border of the constellation.

Fig. 47 shows the constellations around the South Pole, which is situated in Octans. There is no bright star close to this pole of the sky, the nearest being a sixth magnitude. The figure shows the positions of five of the first magnitude stars—Canopus, Achernar, α Crucis, α and β Centauri.

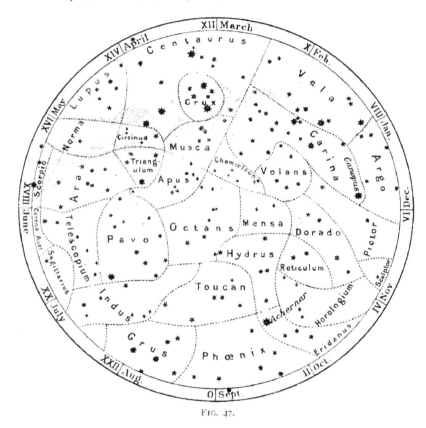

FIG. 47.

The constellation Crux, or the Southern Cross, is of small dimensions, but brilliant, and in a neighbourhood containing a good many bright stars. The Cross is formed of the four stars α 0·9 magnitude, β 1·6, γ 2·0, and δ 3·4 magnitudes. Of these, α is a triple star, the companions being a second and a sixth magnitude; and γ a double, with a companion of the fifth magnitude. The constellation also contains a cluster of stars, several of which are red.

The constellation Argo Navis, owing to its great extent, has been divided for convenience of reference into four separate constellations—Carina, the keel;

Vela, the sails; Puppis, the stern; and Malus, the mast. It contains many objects of interest, and a rich part of the Milky Way passes through it. One of its most remarkable stars is the curious variable η, which is surrounded by a great diffused nebula, with dark markings crossing it. Though η was previously noticed as a variable, Sir John Herschel first called special attention to it in 1837, when he observed it to have increased to nearly three times its former brilliancy. It was then brighter than Rigel, but soon declined somewhat, only to blaze out with still greater splendour in 1843, when it was nearly equal to Sirius. At this brightness it remained, with some fluctuations up to 1850. In 1865 it was only of the fifth magnitude.

Near the star α Centauri the Milky Way divides into two streams, with a broad space between them, in which comparatively few stars are to be seen. This star is a splendid binary, the principal star 0·2 magnitude, and the companion about the third. The period of their revolution round their common centre of gravity has been estimated at from seventy-seven to eighty-eight years by different authorities. A cluster, which has been described as one of the finest in the sky, is known as ω Centauri. It consists of a large number of stars, the brightest of which are of about the ninth magnitude. More than 6000 stars have been counted on a photograph of this cluster. Two other clusters will be found in the constellation Toucan, in which the Nebecula Minor is also situated. The latter, as well as the Nebecula Major, in Dorado, look like outlying patches of the Milky Way.

The Milky Way can be traced as a great band of stars completely encircling the celestial vault. The small maps introduced into the text show only the brightest portions of it. Its course can be followed by the reader more in detail on the larger maps on Plates XII., XIV., XV., and XVI. Commencing with the northern section on Plate XV., it will be seen to pass through Perseus, where it envelopes the "festoon," the most conspicuous portion of that constellation. The bright stars of Cassiopeia are also involved in it. From this point it crosses the southern part of Cepheus, where one of the darker patches, to be found occasionally in different regions of the Milky Way, presents itself. The next constellation it embraces is Cygnus, where there is another dark patch, and a little farther on the great bifurcation begins. The extension of this most remarkable feature of the Galaxy will be well seen on Plate XIV. The two distinct streams can be followed across Vulpecula and Sagitta, and into Aquila, the western branch ending in Ophiuchus, while the eastern branch pursues its course across Sagittarius and into the south polar constellations. In Scorpio the western branch re-establishes itself, and the Galaxy again consists of two streams of irregular form, separated by a dark interval, crossed here and there by branches of greater or less breadth. We now reach the part of the Milky Way which is not visible from middle northern latitudes. In Scorpio the Galaxy attains its greatest breadth, one branch passing through Lupus. The separate branches can be further traced as far as α Centauri, where the two streams join, and continue their united course to the "Southern Cross," all the bright stars of which are enveloped in it. A very remarkable feature of this part of the Galaxy is the "Coal-sack," a dark oval patch almost devoid of stars. It contains, indeed, only one naked-eye star within its bounds, but the telescope shows a number of small points of light. Passing the Coal-sack the stream narrows at its entrance to the constellation Argo, but soon again widens out

I

into the most diffused part of the whole stream. It is here broken up by irregular openings, one of which almost completely crosses the stream at right angles. The remainder of its course will be followed on Plate XII. from the point where it again becomes visible from our northern latitudes. This is the least bright part of the Galaxy. Leaving Argo it enters Monoceros, passing between Orion and Canis Minor without enveloping any of the bright stars of these constellations. From this it passes into Auriga and on to Perseus, the point from which we started.

On Plate IX. will be found Sir Wm. Herschel's section of the Milky Way, illustrating his idea of the distribution of the stars in space. He supposed that the universe of stars which we see around us is distributed within the bounds of a widely extended but comparatively thin layer, with the sun not very far from the centre. Looking into space, either in the direction of A or C—that is, at right angles to the diameter of the layer, or irregular plate—we meet a small number of stars in our line of sight. On the other hand, if we look along the diameter towards B or F, we see a vast multitude of stars, forming what appears, to our sight, as the Galaxy, or Milky Way. The bifurcation, which has been referred to, beginning at α Cygni and traceable to α Centauri, he accounted for by supposing the existence of a cleft or split in the edge of the stratum, illustrated in his diagram on Plate IX., by the opening ending at E, the two great streams being represented as seen in the directions S D and S F. Herschel's hypothesis of the distribution of the stars has been adopted by most eminent astronomers as the correct view so far as the great majority of the visible stars are concerned, but whether the nebulæ and denser clusters are included within the limits of the Galaxy is not so certain.

INDEX.

PLATES

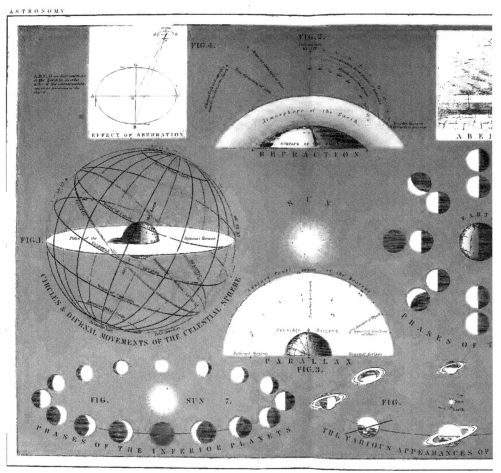

FIG.4.

FIG.2.

EFFECT OF ABERRATION

Atmosphere of the Earth

SURFACE OF

REFRACTION

ABER

S U N

FIG.1.

CIRCLES & DIURNAL MOVEMENTS OF THE CELESTIAL SPHERE

Sensible Horizon

PARALLAX

FIG.3.

PHASES OF T

FIG. SUN 7.

PHASES OF THE INFERIOR PLANETS

FIG.

THE VARIOUS APPEARANCES OF

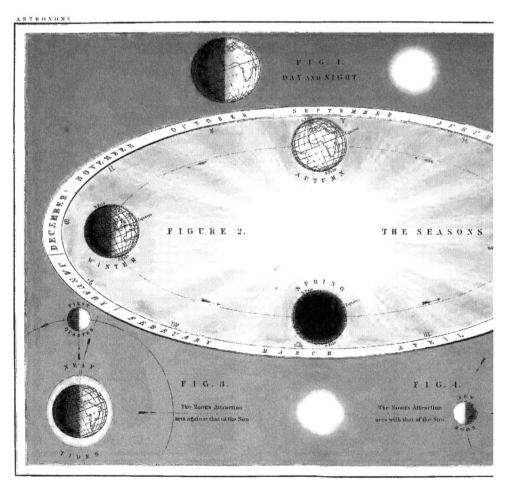

FIG. 1.
DAY AND NIGHT

THE SEASONS

FIGURE 2.

OCTOBER SEPTEMBER AUGUST

NOVEMBRE

DECEMBER

AUTUMN

WINTER

JANUARY FEBRUARY

SPRING

MARCH APRIL

FIRST QUARTER

NEAP

TIDES

FIG. 3.

The Moon's Attraction
acts against that of the Sun

FIG. 4.

The Moon's Attraction
acts with that of the Sun

NEW MOON

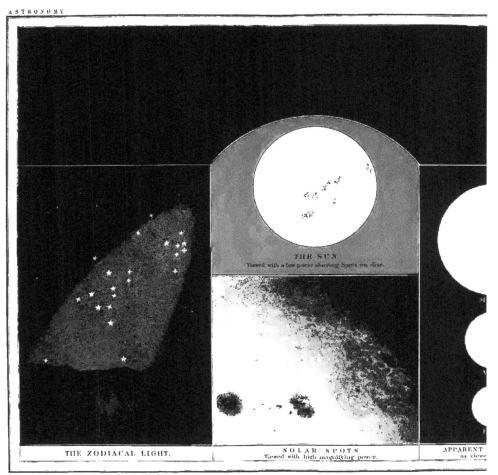

THE ZODIACAL LIGHT.

THE SUN
Viewed with a low power showing Spots on disc.

SOLAR SPOTS
Viewed with high magnifying power.

APPARENT
as view

London Printed and Published by the ...

The Crater Copernicus from
a drawing by Serela.

Enlarged View of the Moon   4 Days old.

PHASES OF

FIG.I.FULL MOON from a drawing in Bode's Jahrbuch 1825.

4 Days.

5 Days.

6 Days.

7¼ Days.

8½ Days.

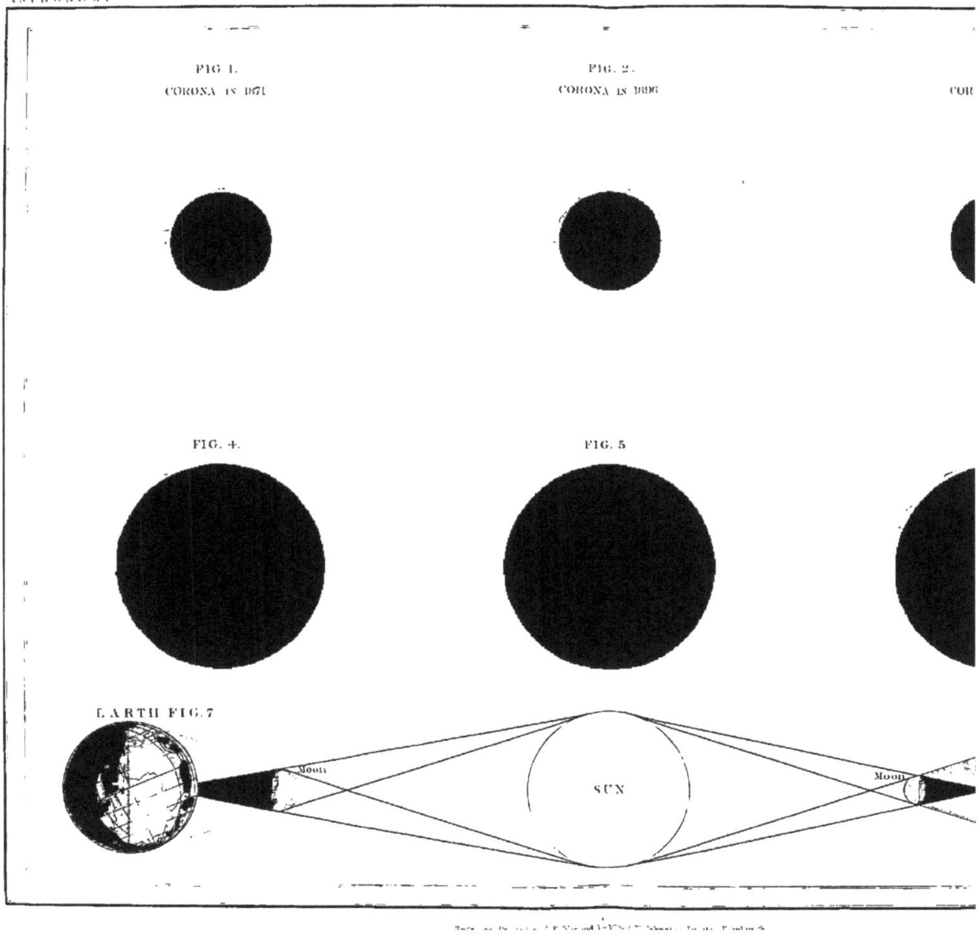

FIG 1.
CORONA IN 1871

FIG. 2.
CORONA IN 1896

COR

FIG. 4.

FIG. 5

EARTH FIG. 7

Moon

SUN

Moon

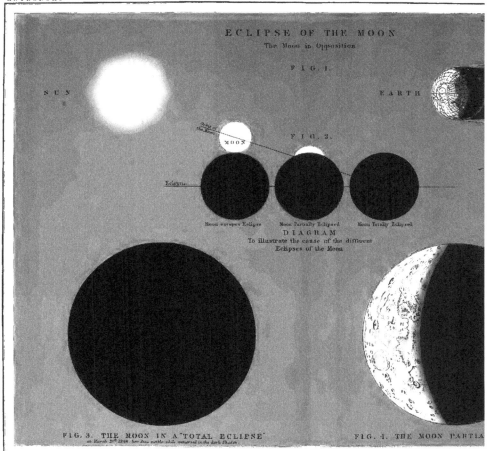

ECLIPSE OF THE MOON
The Moon in Opposition

F I G. 1.

SUN

EARTH

Orbit of
the Moon

MOON

F I G. 2.

Eclipse

Moon escapes Eclipse   Moon Partially Eclipsed   Moon Totally Eclipsed

D I A G R A M
To illustrate the cause of the different
Eclipses of the Moon

FIG. 3. THE MOON IN A "TOTAL ECLIPSE"
on March 21ˢᵗ 1848. her face visible while immersed in the dark Shadow.

FIG. 4. THE MOON PARTIA

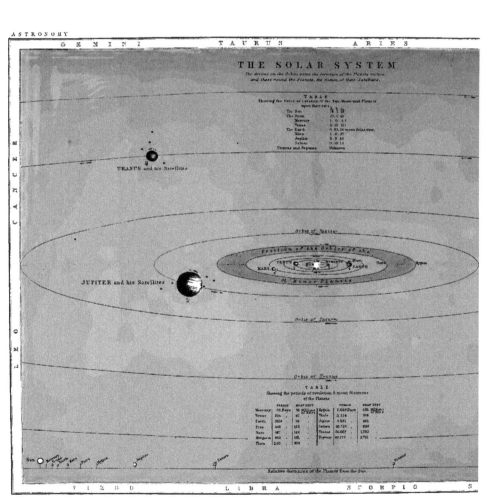

THE SOLAR SYSTEM

The Arrows on the Orbits point the direction of the Planets motion
and those round the Planets, the motion of their Satellites.

TABLE
Showing the times of rotation of the Sun Moon and Planets
upon their axes.

	d	h	m
The Sun			
The Moon	29	1	40
Mercury	1	0	5.4
Venus	0	23	21
The Earth	0	23	56 mean Solar time.
Mars	1	0	37
Jupiter	0	9	55
Saturn	0	10	16
Uranus and Neptune	Unknown		

URANUS and his Satellites

Orbit of Uranus

REGION OF THE ORBITS OF THE

Minor Planets

VESTA JUNO SUN EARTH
MARS CERES Venus Mercury Hygea

JUPITER and his Satellites

Orbit of Saturn

Orbit of Neptune

TABLE
Showing the periods of revolution & mean distances
of the Planets

	PERIOD in Days	MEAN DIST in Millions		PERIOD	MEAN DIST in Millions
Mercury	88	37	Ceres	7,008 Days	238
Venus	224	69	Vesta	3,514	996
Earth	365	96	Jupiter	4,332	985
Juno	448	133	Saturn	10,759	896
Mars	687	144	Uranus	30,687	1,822
Hygea	882	161	Neptune	60,177	2,792
Ceres	1,193	264			

Sun Mercury Venus Earth Mars Jupiter Saturn Uranus Neptune

Relative distances of the Planets from the Sun

Drawn & Engraved and Published by W & A K Johnston Limited Edinburgh

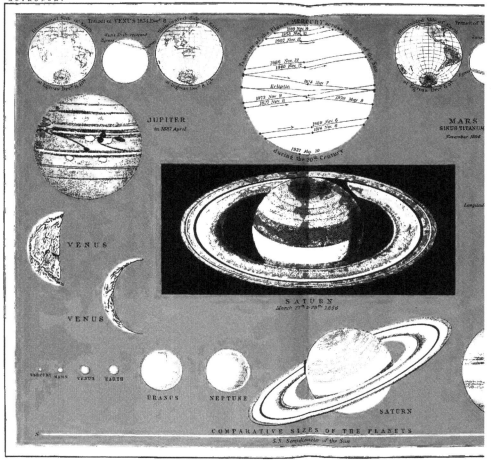

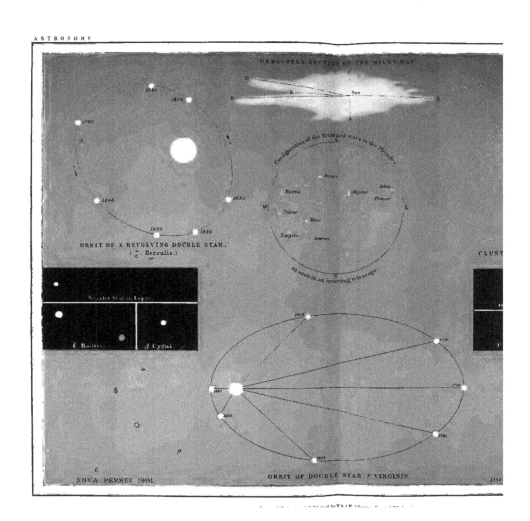

HERSCHEL'S SECTION OF THE MILKY WAY

Configuration of the Principal Stars in the Pleiades.

Merope

Electra   Alcyone   Maia

Celeno   Asterope   Pleione

Taygeta   Maia

Atlas

as seen in an inverting telescope.

ORBIT OF A REVOLVING DOUBLE STAR,
[ζ Herculis.]

Scarlet Star in Lepus.

ε Boötis.   β Cygni.

NOVA PERSEI 1901.   ORBIT OF DOUBLE STAR γ VIRGINIS

CLUST

TRACK OF METEORS
Observed at the Royal Observatory Greenwich
November 13. 14. 1866.

.

Engraved, Printed and Published by W & A K Johnston Limited Edinburgh

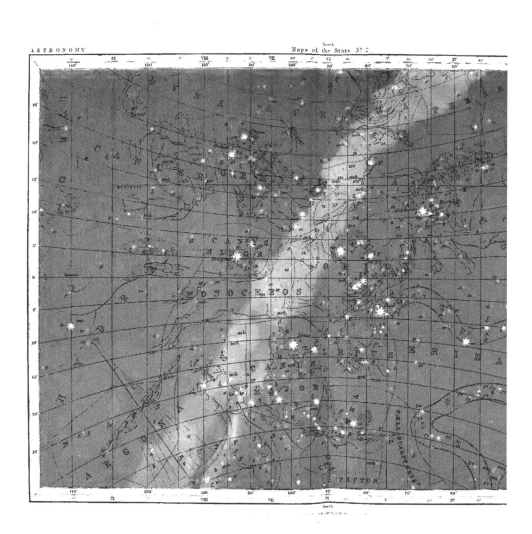

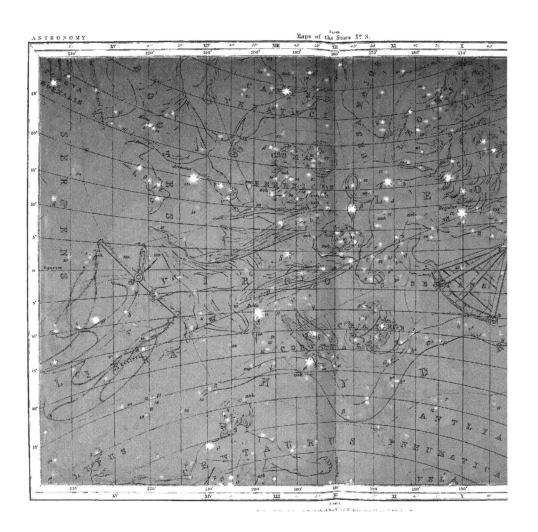

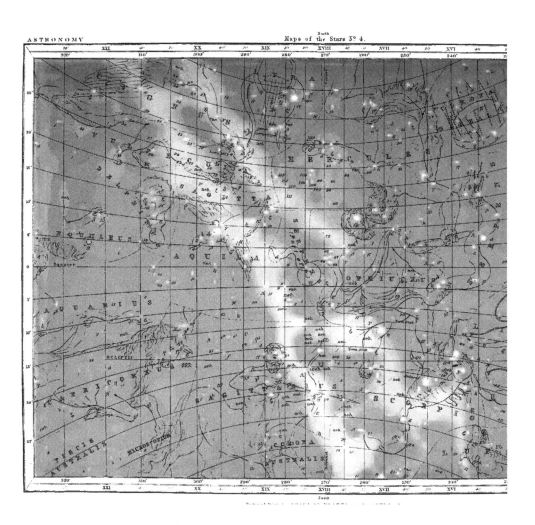

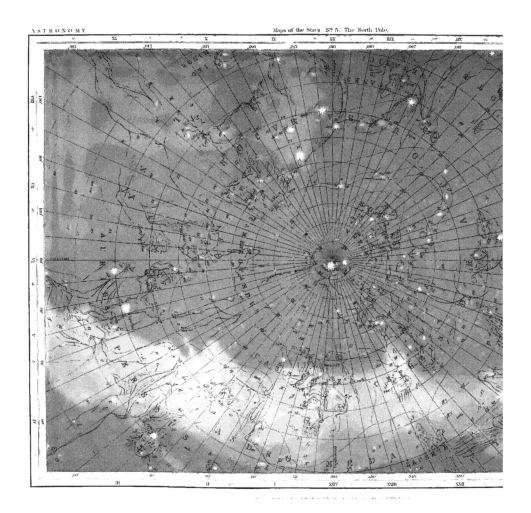

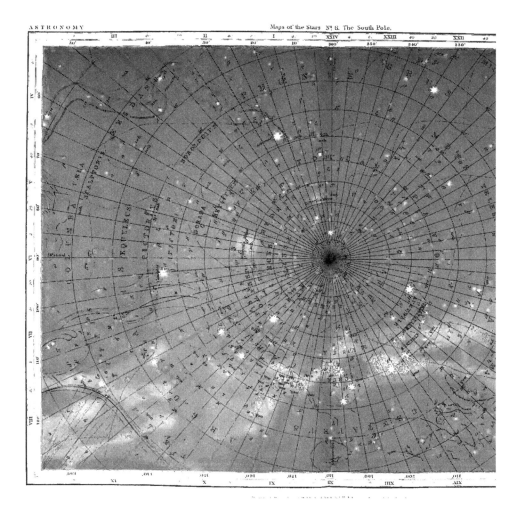

DATE DUE	BORROWER'S NAME	
	Anne Knowles 17 Feb. 99	5994

Lightning Source UK Ltd.
Milton Keynes UK
UKHW022347270120
357710UK00006B/334